⮞ The Angel
and the Serpent

The Angel
and the Serpent

THE STORY OF NEW HARMONY

by William E. Wilson

INDIANA UNIVERSITY PRESS
Bloomington and Indianapolis

This book is a publication of

Indiana University Press
601 North Morton Street
Bloomington, IN 47404-3797 USA

http://www.indiana.edu/~iupress

Telephone orders 800-842-6796
Fax orders 812-855-7931
Orders by email iuporder@indiana.edu

The paper used in this publication meets the minimum requirements
of American National Standard for Information Sciences—Permanence
of Paper for Printed Library Materials, ANSI Z39.48-1984.

Manufactured in the United States of America

LCCN 64-10827
ISBN 0-253-10360-6 (clothbound)
ISBN 0-253-20326-0 (paperback)

4 5 6 7 8 02 01 00 99 98

For Ellen

CONTENTS

ILLUSTRATIONS

(following page 50)

George Rapp, the founder of the Harmony Society
Rapp's home in Iptingen, Württemberg
Rapp's home in Harmonie, Indiana
Frame church at Harmonie, Indiana, in 1819
North doorway of the Harmonists' brick church
A Harmonist dwelling
"Footprints" in limestone at New Harmony
The sundial of the Harmony Society
Dormitory No. 2 with the sundial on the wall
The Harmonists' fire engine, "the Pat Lyons"
Harmonist wagon, built in 1823

(following page 114)

Robert Owen, the founder of the Community of Equality
A view of New Lanark
A drawing of the phalanstery, as Owen visualized it
The sons of Robert Owen: Robert Dale Owen, William Owen,
    David Dale Owen, Richard Owen
Map of New Harmony, 1825
Harmonie on the Wabash
The Boatload of Knowledge, sketched by Charles-Alexandre
    Lesueur

(following page 146)

Drawings of the Harmonists' frame and brick churches, renamed
    the Steeple House and the Hall of New Harmony, by David
    Dale Owen and Charles-Alexandre Lesueur

ILLUSTRATIONS

Thespian Society theatre ticket

New Harmony scenes, sketched by Charles-Alexandre Lesueur and
David Dale Owen

Charles-Alexandre Lesueur, a watercolor by Karl Bodmer

Another sketch of Lesueur by Bodmer

New Harmony in 1832, a watercolor by Karl Bodmer

Some important members of the Community of Equality: William
Maclure, Thomas Say, Frances Wright, Madame Marie
Duclos Fretageot, Joseph Neef

(following page 194)

The Rapp-Maclure house in New Harmony

Joseph Neef's home

The Fauntleroy Home

David Dale Owen's laboratory

Wagons of Captain Alfred Ribeyre, the corn king

The New Harmony opera house

New Harmony Centennial parade

A Golden Rain tree

Restored Harmonist house

Mrs. Kenneth D. Owen and Paul Tillich at the dedication of
"The Cave of the New Being" in Paul Tillich Park, 1963

The Roofless Church in New Harmony

PREFACE

Contrary to popular belief, a writer seldom has to search for a subject. Usually he is in full flight from a dozen subjects that have been pursuing him for years. To begin his next book, he has only to stop, turn in his tracks, and resolutely face one of his pursuers. At that point, however, the chase is resumed in the opposite direction, for subjects are coy as well as importunate and they turn in their own tracks and flee when an author is ready to capitulate. A second race has to be run, sometimes as long as the first, before a subject becomes a book.

The subject of this book began its pursuit of me when I was a small boy. Sitting on the front porches of my numerous aunts and uncles in New Harmony listening to their stories of the past, I was already in flight, for I imagined "Rappites" and "Owenites" then as something like them, their friends, their contemporaries, rocking on front porches, fanning themselves with palm-leaf fans that advertised the Posey County Fair, endlessly reminiscent. As I played with children descended from the men and women who had made the town's past and, later, danced and went to parties with them in ancient houses that the founders of New Harmony had constructed, I recognized in my young companions a rebellion against the older generation similar to my own. We, after all, were of the new century. We had our own history to make.

After I grew up and left southern Indiana, the flight continued, for writing became my profession and I knew that New Harmony was a subject that badly needed writing about. More disturbing still to my conscience was the knowledge that, in my heart, I wanted to write about it. "Rappites" and "Owenites," as my uncles and aunts called them, had become for me at last real people.

On several occasions, I turned briefly, faced my pursuer, and tried to placate both it and my conscience by devoting a few chapters to New Harmony in a book I was working on or writing an article about the town for a magazine. But I had no intention then of losing myself in the forest of conflicting myths and stubbornly elusive facts that I knew I must penetrate before I could arrive at the truth about Rapps and Owens. Other subjects were pursuing me that seemed easier to capture. New Harmony was a book that would require long and arduous research and a full scholarly treatment, and I never seemed to have the time.

Probably I should never have stopped and begun a pursuit of the subject of New Harmony in real earnest if I had not returned to Indiana a dozen or so years ago to make my home in my native state. Even so, I might not have succumbed to the fascination of the subject if the Director of the Indiana University Press had not joined forces with my pursuer and begun a subtle campaign of calling me up periodically and saying, as if the idea had just occurred to him for the first time, "Have you ever thought of writing a book about New Harmony?" One day, finally, I surprised both myself and him by replying, "Yes; I will commence tomorrow." At once, the chase in the opposite direction began.

To Bernard B. Perry, therefore, Director of the Indiana University Press, I make my first acknowledgment in this preface, because in the course of time he and New Harmony together eventually caught up with me.

Others at Indiana University to whom I am especially indebted for their kindness and helpfulness while I was working on this book are: Dean John W. Ashton, Vice President for

Graduate Development, Professors C. L. Barber, Edwin H. Cady, Philip B. Daghlian, Wadie Jwaideh, Herbert J. Muller, J. Albert Robbins, Oscar O. Winther, and Dr. Elfrieda Lang.

Those associated with other institutions and other places who have been of assistance to me are: Professor Julian P. Boyd, Editor of the Papers of Thomas Jefferson, Princeton University; Professor Richard M. Cameron of Boston University; Professor Henry Steele Commager of Amherst College; Dr. John H. Fisher, Secretary of the Modern Language Association; Dr. Oliver W. Holmes, Executive Director of the National Historical Commission, National Archives, Washington, D.C.; Dr. and Mrs. Charles M. James of Philadelphia; Dr. and Mrs. Paul A. Bishop of Philadelphia; Professor Russel B. Nye of Michigan State University; Professor Howard A. Wilson of Knox College; Mr. J. W. Forsyth, Librarian, Carnegie Library, Ayr, Scotland; Mr. A. Inglis, General Manager, The Gourock Ropework Co., Ltd., New Lanark Mills, Lanark, Scotland; and M. André Maury, Conservateur du Muséum d'Histoire Naturelle du Havre, France.

As I worked in New Harmony, I became indebted to Mr. Don Blair for sharing with me his lively curiosity about the town's past and his detailed knowledge of the architecture of Harmonist buildings; to Mrs. Mary Aline Bradley, Librarian of the New Harmony Workingmen's Institute, for her tireless and cheerful helpfulness in the library; and to Mr. Kenneth Dale Owen for permission to examine manuscripts in his home and to publish one of them.

For assistance in my research I thank the efficient staffs of the Indiana University Library and its branches in Geology and Biology, the Lilly Library of Indiana University, the Archives of Purdue University, the Library of the New Harmony Workingmen's Institute, the Museum of Old Economy in Ambridge, Pennsylvania, the Library of the American Philosophical Society, the Indiana State Library, the Indiana Historical Society

PREFACE

Library, the Library of the Historical Society of Pennsylvania, and the Robert Lee Blaffer Trust of New Harmony.

I wish to pay tribute to my wife, Ellen, for her reading and criticism of the manuscript and for enduring patiently with me the long and sometimes frustrating period of the research and writing, and to thank my sons—William, for his counsel regarding the geological aspects of the subject; Douglas, for a reading and criticism of the semifinal draft of the manuscript; and Cameron, for contributing to my understanding of the flora and fauna of the region.

This book was written with the support of a grant from the American Philosophical Society, a grant for research assistance from the Graduate Research Division of the Indiana University Graduate School, and a Fulbright grant for travel to and from Europe. To the administrators of these organizations I am profoundly grateful.

WILLIAM E. WILSON

Indiana University
Bloomington, Indiana

✎ The Angel
and the Serpent

Part One

❧§❧

Harmonie

1

IN HIS thirtieth year, George Rapp began to speak in his own
house. That house, in the village of Iptingen in southwestern Germany, bore little resemblance to the domestic architecture that Rapp and his followers would create thirty years later
in southwestern Indiana, the houses that still make New Harmony, Indiana, unique among Middle Western villages. It
stood at the edge of the street, as do New Harmony's houses,
and there was no front door, the entrance, like the entrances of
the Germans' later homes in New Harmony, being at the side.
But in all other respects it was different, a tall, drafty, high-
gabled house with plastered walls and exposed timbers, a dark
narrow house, like the other peasant homes in Iptingen, ill-
suited to the gathering of large numbers of people.

To this house the pious of Iptingen began to come on Sundays to hear George Rapp talk about the Bible; and as his reputation for wisdom and eloquence spread throughout the region,
others soon appeared for those Sunday meetings, coming from
Wiernsheim, Gärtringen, Ehringen, and Nufringen nearby, and
from Schnaid and Winterbach, which were farther away, and
attendance in the established church began to fall of noticeably.

The essence of Rapp's argument for separate religious services was that the established church of Germany had become a
Babel. The church was no longer of God, he said; it was of the

Devil. Parsons ate, drank, and fattened their bellies with no thought of the poor. Their sermons were no longer sermons; they were only lectures that ignored the teachings of Jesus Christ and interpreted the historic records of the Old Testament as myths. The parsons talked of Progress and Reason, instead of Christian virtue and God's will. Often they devoted the holy service to discourses on the raising of cattle, bees, and fruit. As for the music of the church, the words and tunes of the old hymns had been changed beyond recognition and resembled the oratorios and cantatas of the beer gardens.

Such were Sundays in George Rapp's high-gabled house in Iptingen. On Mondays, the villagers and farmers who came to hear him were often in jail, charged with absence from the services of the established church, charged with attending unauthorized meetings, charged with failure to pay their tithes. And on more than one occasion George Rapp himself was in jail with them.

Why did he persist in his offenses against the church? the judges of Württemberg asked George Rapp.

Because, Rapp replied, he had found the fountainhead of religion for himself and its substance was in Jesus Christ.

Did he believe in the principles of the Christian church? they asked him.

Yes, he said; but the church had lost sight of these principles in the luxury and confusion of its ceremonies. Anyone who could repeat the catechism was permitted to take part in the sacraments; but communicants learned the catechism only by rote, and it had lost its meaning. At confirmations children were allowed to think more of the clothes they wore than of the ritual they were engaged in.

So George Rapp persisted, and as time passed he became more and more defiant.

This man, the spiritual leader of the Germans who founded Harmonie, Indiana, in 1814, was a remarkable man, born

Johann Georg Rapp in the village of Iptingen, in the bailiwick of Maulbronn, Württemberg, on the twenty-eighth day of October, 1757. His father, Adam Rapp, was a farmer and vine-planter.

Although early in life George Rapp demonstrated a superior intelligence that fitted him for something better than manual labor, he went to work in the fields when he finished his common-school education. This choice of vocation was almost inevitable in a country essentially agricultural, famous for fruits and grains and potatoes, and where a class system of many generations was practically inviolable in spite of a tradition of democracy as strong as any in Germany at that time. Rapp became a vinedresser, a specialist in pruning and training and cultivating the plants his father was skilled in setting out.

At the age of twenty-four he wooed and married a farmer's daughter named Christina Benzinger. He was a handsome youth then, somewhat heavy featured, but six feet tall, powerfully built, blue-eyed, and with a fine resounding musical voice. Christina bore him a son, John, whom George Rapp outlived, as he would outlive Christina herself and as he would outlive another son that he would adopt in middle age. Christina also bore him a daughter, Rosina, who would survive her father by only two years. In fact, George Rapp was to retain his physical and mental vigor until the day of his death, within a few months of his ninetieth birthday.

Although Rapp's formal schooling came to a close when he was still a boy, he remained a student the rest of his life, meditating principally upon the works of theologians and philosophers. He was strongly influenced by the thinking of Friedrich Jacobi, the philosopher, of Friedrich Schleiermacher, the theologian and Protestant pastor, and of Johann Heinrich Jung-Stilling, the Swedenborgian; but more and more, as the years passed, he read the works of Johann von Herder.

Herder regarded men as integral parts of the world in which

they lived, and not as separate individuals. To him God was a living ever-present person, and not an abstraction. Possibly in the beginning it was Johann von Herder's love of folksong that attracted George Rapp, for Rapp was himself a man of musical talent who composed hymns that simple men and women could understand and enjoy. From that original interest the progression to Herder's later philosophical writing would have been only natural.

It is Herder's influence that is most evident in George Rapp's one venture into formal philosophical writing of his own—an attempt to expound his socio-religious thinking in a book published at Harmonie in 1824. *Gedanken über die Bestimmung des Menschen* Rapp called this book, or "Thoughts on the Destiny of Man." In the title there is a resemblance to Herder's *Ideen zur Philosophie der Geschichte des Menscheit* perhaps. Certainly there is a similarity in the ideas the two books express, although Rapp's language is unliterary and the marshaling of his thoughts is haphazard compared with Herder's style and order.

In religion, George Rapp was a Lutheran, and by his own definition of Lutheranism he would have argued that he was a true Lutheran. Like Luther, he believed that the final authority of every man's faith was the Bible. Like Luther, he was convinced that salvation was the free gift of God through Christ and that this gift was offered directly and should not be received through any human mediator. Also like Luther, he contended that if everyone were truly Christian there would be no need for civil government. But neither Rapp nor Luther ever arrived at a point where they thought everyone was truly Christian, and until that happy day of perfection it seemed to them best to have a few men like themselves in charge, alongside the civil authorities.

Submission to civil authority, Rapp argued, was an act of

man's love for other men. But he believed with Luther that the civil government had no right to interfere with the spiritual life of the individual, and every Christian individual was privileged to preach and administer the sacraments if he wished and when necessary. He thought every church community should choose pastors to perform these functions under normal circumstances; but, being of strong will and superior intelligence, he shared Luther's misgivings about the peasants' ability to govern the church from within. What it came down to, as Rapp later practiced his religion, was faith in the individual so long as the individual agreed with George Rapp and followed him.

Had George Rapp lived in the Seventeenth Century he would certainly have taken part in the Pietist "revival of the true religion," but he can not accurately be called a Pietist, as he is sometimes labeled, because he was born too late for that form of Puritanism. He was, rather, a follower of the leaders of another Protestant revival subsequent to Pietism—men like Herder, Jacobi, and Schleiermacher. At the beginning, George Rapp was not even a Separatist, like some of the pious around him. For a long time he kept his disapproval of the established church to himself and conformed to the religious practices of his village. But in his thirtieth year he could no longer contain his inner protests and, like the Pietist leaders of a century before his time, he began to speak in his own house, persisting in defiance of the judges of Württemberg.

In 1799, George Rapp was fined for purchasing a herd of swine and driving them through the streets on Good Friday while the church was holding morning services. That service, he told his judges, was an empty show. It was better to buy swine and drive them home on a holy day than to take part in such a sacrilege. Furthermore, the swine were a good bargain that a poor man could not afford to pass up. Had his judges forgotten the Scriptures?

THE ANGEL AND THE SERPENT

*What man shall there be among you, that shall have one
sheep, and if it fall into a pit on the sabbath day, will he not
lay hold on it, and lift it out?*

Already George Rapp had come to believe what he would
argue in essence later in his *Gedanken:* namely, that the Lord
helps those who help themselves.

Still, Rapp was not so fanatic as some of the dissenters of the
past and of his own time. Like Luther, he urged his followers to
pay their taxes, rendering unto Caesar the things which were
Caesar's; and, for this reason, the Duke of Württemberg was
inclined to turn a deaf ear to the frequent complaints of the
church authorities against the man from Iptingen. Even when
George Rapp was defiant he was not disrespectful. Unlike some
of the Duke's unruly subjects—one Johannes Goesele in particular, who insulted Napoleon when he came to Württemberg
on a visit—George Rapp knew when to doff his hat and drop
the familiar *du.* Nor did he call himself "Christ's Messenger,"
as Thomas Müntzer had done, or aspire to a crown, like John of
Leyden, "King of the New Jerusalem, Messiah of the Last
Days," *né* Bockelson. Nor was he foolishly inciting his people to
abandon their homes and take off for places like Russia and
America as some religious zealots of his day were doing. At least,
not yet he wasn't. So long as the man paid his taxes, the Duke of
Württemberg reasoned, let him believe as he pleased. He was a
solid, hard-working citizen who seemed to want only to be let
alone and to read the Bible in his own way.

But being let alone and reading the Bible in his own way
were not all that George Rapp wanted. Once he had acquired a
following, he wanted his followers to live as he believed it
pleased God they should live—in harmony with one another,
equal in their stations in life, their property possessed in common. He had taken to heart the thirty-second verse of the fourth
chapter of The Acts: *And the multitude of them that believed
were of one heart and one soul: neither said any of them that*

ought of the things he possessed was his own; but they had all things common. If the Duke of Württemberg had known about this turn in Rapp's thinking, he might have taken stronger measures against his subject.

In his deep resonant voice George Rapp was reading aloud in his house on Sundays the first five verses of the twentieth chapter of the Book of Revelation:

1 *And I saw an angel come down from heaven, having the key of the bottomless pit and a great chain in his hand.*

2 *And he laid hold on the dragon, that old serpent, which is the Devil, and Satan, and bound him a thousand years.*

3 *And cast him into the bottomless pit, and shut him up, and set a seal upon him, that he should deceive the nations no more, till the thousand years should be fulfilled: and after that he must be loosed a little season.*

4 *And I saw thrones, and they sat upon them, and judgment was given unto them: and I saw the souls of them that were beheaded for the witness of Jesus, and for the word of God, and which had not worshipped the beast, neither his image, neither had received his mark upon their foreheads, or in their hands; and they lived and reigned with Christ a thousand years.*

5 *But the rest of the dead lived not again until the thousand years were finished. This is the first resurrection.*

Rapp believed so firmly in a millennium arriving in his own lifetime that on the day of his death, a half century later, he is reported to have said: "If I did not so fully believe that the Lord has designed me to place our society before His presence in the Land of Canaan, I would consider this day my last."

Unlike most chiliasts before him, George Rapp thought of the millennium as an event that men had to prepare for, not a festive excursion to the Holy Land with God supplying the meat and drink and transportation. In Rapp's opinion, the kingdom of heaven was to be reached by man's own efforts here

on earth. In other words, the Lord helps those who help themselves, but only if they help each other too.

In school, George Rapp had studied reading, writing, and
arithmetic, but also geography, and that subject had never
ceased to interest him. He was not, of course, a man who
dreamed of faraway places for adventure's sake; he dreamed of
godliness and the millennium. Therefore, when his beliefs were
clearly defined regarding the way the millennium was to be prepared for, travel began to mean to him a quest for a more con-
genial country where a man could live as he believed God
wanted him to.

It was the reading of a book about Louisiana that inspired
the journey Rapp finally made to America. He might indeed
have gone to Louisiana, instead of Pennsylvania and, later,
Indiana, if he had not first inquired of the French government
about that colony and learned that the French had recently sold
it to the United States. When he inquired further about it
among Dutch merchants who traded with America, their description of the new republic convinced him that the kind of
millennium he envisioned had a better hope of fulfillment in
the North than in the South. There could be no harmony in a
society founded upon Negro slavery.

Meantime, although the Duke of Württemberg continued to
refuse to take stern measures against Rapp's people, the clergy
continued to harass them, stirring up mayors and burgesses
against them, until the arrests, trials, fines, and prison sentences
became intolerable; and after the turn of the century the new
menace of Napoleonic conscriptions was added to these persecu-
tions. Finally, in 1803, George Rapp made up his mind; he
would lead his people out of Germany; he would seek a place
for them in the New World.

Selling his property in Iptingen, he left his wife and daughter
and his flock in the care of an able and ambitious young architect and stonecutter named Frederick Reichert and set off for

America. With him went his son John, who had been certified as a licensed surveyor in Iptingen the year before, and a fellow Separatist named Frederick Conrad Haller, who also wanted to establish a colony of *émigrés*. They traveled by boat down the Rhine and sailed from Amsterdam on the ship *Canton,* arriving at Philadelphia on October 7, 1803.

In the search for land that followed, the three men traveled through Maryland and Pennsylvania and penetrated as far west as Tuscarawas County in Ohio, where Joseph Bimeler, another Württemberg dissenter, would establish Zoar a few years later. Frederick Conrad Haller was most attracted by central Pennsylvania, but George Rapp was drawn to the Ohio River Valley, which reminded him of the Rhine. Finally, in Butler County, Pennsylvania, the man from Iptingen arranged to purchase from a man named Detmar Basse four thousand five hundred acres of land adjacent to the village of Zelienople. This tract was twenty-six miles northwest of Pittsburgh and twelve miles from the Ohio on Connoquenessing Creek. Rapp had brought with him two thousand gulden, or about $800; the land that he contracted to purchase cost $11,250.

"You must not urge anyone to come," he wrote back to Frederick Reichert, telling his lieutenant what he had done; "it is a long and perilous journey."

Not only was the journey long and perilous, the land he had chosen was far removed from anything resembling the civilization his people knew in Germany and the clearing and cultivation of it and the building of a town would require great hardship and self-denial. Nevertheless, eight hundred and thirty-nine men, women, and children in Württemberg undertook the journey.

Three hundred of them arrived at Baltimore on the *Aurora* on the Fourth of July, 1804, a holiday they would always celebrate thereafter with music and free beer for their neighbors as well as themselves. Two hundred and sixty-nine, including

Frederick Reichert, landed at Philadelphia on the *Atlantic* on September 15 of the same year. Four days later, seventy more disembarked at Philadelphia from the *Margaret*. Of this last contingent the majority went with Haller to Lycoming County, Pennsylvania.

Eighty of the sturdiest of Rapp's pilgrims made their way at once with Rapp and his son and Frederick Reichert to Butler County and set to work clearing land and building temporary log houses. Meantime, those who stayed behind in the East were looked after by Germans already established in the New World. Homes were opened to the immigrants. Food and clothing were shared. The German Society of Philadelphia collected two hundred dollars and gave it to the Württembergers to tide them over until George Rapp was ready to call them to their new home. That time came, finally, in February, 1805.

2

In the Museum of Old Economy, in what is now Ambridge, Pennsylvania, where the Württembergers established their third and final community in America, there is a document called "The Articles of Association 1805," bound in a volume entitled *Book of Life*. This document gives the name "Harmonie" to the town in Butler County to which George Rapp called his followers as soon as there was adequate housing for them; it is dated February 15, 1805; and it bears the signatures of the Württembergers who formed the first community. These Articles of Association are the basic agreement of the Harmony Society, and that agreement remained virtually unchanged in the nine subsequent contracts that were drawn up in the course of the society's one-hundred-year history.

Under the terms of this contract, the Harmonists gave all their real and personal property to "George Rapp and his associates" for the benefit and use of the community and placed it at Rapp's full disposal. They agreed to submit to the rules and regulations that George Rapp and his associates established in order to promote the common welfare, and in return George Rapp and his associates made several promises. They would extend to each member of the community and his family the privilege of attending every religious meeting and of receiving for himself and his family "all such instruction in church and school as may be reasonably required." They would also supply the members and their families with "all the necessaries of life, such as clothing, meat, drink, lodging, etc.," for the well and for the sick, for the aged and those unfit for labor, and for the children of those parents who should die.

If a member wished to withdraw from the community after signing this contract, it was agreed that he would renounce all claims to compensations or wages for his labor, but the value of the property he had brought to the community would be refunded to him without interest in annual installments, as George Rapp and his associates should determine. If the withdrawing member had brought nothing to the community, he would receive money in proportion to the length of his stay, his conduct in the community, and the amount his necessities should require, again as George Rapp and his associates should determine.

By common consent George Rapp was already the spiritual leader of the society. His choice of business manager was Frederick Reichert because of the ability Frederick had demonstrated in holding the group together in Germany during Rapp's absence, in enlisting recruits, and in getting everybody safely transported to America. It was a wise choice.

Immediately Frederick Reichert divided the activities of the community into seven departments and appointed a manager for each department. These managers were directly responsible to him, and thus he was able to keep a close watch over the society's affairs and to decide quickly which of their endeavors were profitable and which were not.

About this time Reichert, two months short of his thirtieth birthday, changed his name to Frederick Rapp and became George Rapp's adopted son. By this time, George Rapp was known to everyone in the community as "Father Rapp," although he was only forty-eight years old.

In spite of hardships, progress and prosperity in the Pennsylvania community began at once. In the first year, one hundred and fifty acres were cleared and the Harmonists built a church, a mill, a large barn, and several more log houses. In the second year, their labors added four hundred more acres of land to the clearing, a sawmill, a tannery, a distillery, a brick storehouse, and a vineyard of four acres. By 1809, the fourth year, they were harvesting six thousand bushels of Indian corn, four thousand five hundred of wheat, four thousand five hundred of rye, ten thousand bushels of potatoes, four thousand pounds of flax, and fifty gallons of sweet oil made from the poppy. In 1810, they constructed a woolen mill and began to raise merino sheep from a flock of one hundred that they had bought from a Yankee named Hopkins. That year, only five years after they arrived on the banks of Connoquenessing Creek, two thousand acres were in cultivation and one hundred and thirty buildings of brick, frame, and logs housed the seven hundred members of the society.

But happiness, unlike progress and prosperity, is not a matter of statistics. Two events in the history of the society during their first years in Pennsylvania are evidence that all was not so well in Harmonie as the foregoing figures suggest.

The first of these events was a journey George Rapp made to Washington, D.C., in 1806, less than a year after the signing of the Articles of Association. On January 6 of that year, he was sitting in the chamber of the United States Senate listening to Senator Samuel Smith of Maryland read a petition (*see Appendix A*) that George Rapp and his associates had laboriously composed and that two hundred and two of the members had signed.

Through the clumsiness of its use of the alien English language, the petition speaks eloquently of the nature of the Harmonists, and by what it leaves unsaid as well as what it says, it reveals the problems that were troubling its leaders. The land they had bought on Connoquenessing Creek was "too small, too brocken & too cold for to raise Vine." They wanted about thirty thousand acres of land "in the western country." For this they could not pay directly but begged the Government to give them reasonable terms, for when they sold their houses and property in Germany they got "Scarce half the value of it" and afterward they had large expenses for travel and most of their people were "unwealthy" to begin with.

In Washington, George Rapp felt lost among so many English-speaking people and ill-at-ease in his simple clothes. He had not brought enough linen with him, and since he had to wear his best clothes every day, he was troubled about the impression he was making among people who gave more importance to cleanliness than anyone he had ever encountered up to that time. Still, it seemed to him that the officials of Washington treated him with respect. Everybody was friendly.

Rapp did not understand legislative procedure any better than he understood English, and he was deceived by the vote he witnessed the first day he was in the Senate. He thought the "ayes" he heard meant that the Harmonist petition was granted and the matter would go immediately to the House, whereas actually the Senate was only approving the appointment of a committee to draw up a bill. According to the *Annals of Congress*, the *Congressional Record* of that period, the bill that finally came out of the committee authorized "location of a quantity of land in the Indiana Territory by George Rapp and his associates, they paying two dollars therefor, and giving them a credit, without interest for six years, when they are to pay one-fourth of the purchase money and the residue in six annual payments." The bill did not receive its first reading in the Senate until ten days after the initial action.

While he waited, George Rapp passed his days and nights taking walks along the Potomac River, writing letters home to Pennsylvania, and composing a hymn of twenty-four verses for his congregation to sing. On the twenty-ninth of January, the Senate gave the bill its third reading and passed it, sending it on to the House; but by that time George Rapp was on his way home. There were quarrels among the people of Harmonie and his presence was needed. In Baltimore, en route, he wrote bitterly to Frederick that he would rather live in disgraceful exile with his family than dwell in an atmosphere of un-Christian disputes in a community supposedly dedicated to preparation for the millennium. But he continued on his journey and set the trouble aright when he got home.

What happened in the House of Representatives when the bill finally reached that legislative body reveals something of the temper of the times and of both the official and popular attitudes toward such groups as George Rapp's Harmonists, of which there were many in America in that period. Opponents of the bill argued hotly against the sale of public lands to foreigners, especially upon such liberal terms as were proposed. It was not fair, they said, to allow aliens to have public lands at prices lower than those offered to veterans of the Revolution. As soon as the word got back to Europe, they said, there would be a wholesale emigration of all the poor of that continent toward the United States. They disapproved of wine culture too, protesting that it would be no addition to the nation's commerce and would gradually undermine the people's health. Wine drinking was for foreigners, anyhow. It was un-American.

If an American wanted to destroy his health, let him drink American whiskey.

On the other hand, those who favored the bill argued that it would be to the nation's advantage to encourage devout and hard-working people to develop the western lands. They read their Bibles, didn't they, even if they did speak an unintelligible gibberish and produce a beverage that was not one-hundred-per-cent red-white-and-blue-ruin? Such people would be a good example for others in the region where they settled. America could do with a little more piety and morality. Americans were getting morally soft.

The bill squeaked by the first vote, 51 to 50. It passed the second reading too. The third reading came on February 14.

Representative John G. Jackson of Virginia opened the final debate by reminding the House that the land in question had formerly belonged to the state he represented and that the Union held it only in trust. The House had no right to parcel it out to a flock of foreigners without Virginia's consent, he said. At that point, Representative John Smilie of Pennsylvania rose to his feet and retorted that Mr. Jackson's state laid claim to every inch of land up to the North Pole and, for his part, he was getting sick and tired of asking Virginia's permission every time the Federal Government wanted to build a dam or a bridge.

"We can hardly turn around without somehow invading the rights of Virginia," Mr. Smilie said.

Representative William Ely of Massachusetts seemed to go along wih Mr. Smilie's views. He agreed that more piety and morality were needed in the nation, especially in those regions west of Massachusetts. And he failed to see where Virginia's rights were involved. But from that position he was suddenly arguing that it would be a mistake to settle these Germans all in one place, where they could become clannish and exclude others. They should buy many small tracts of land scattered all over the United States, so that their influence would be wide-spread. In short, he was against the bill as it stood. The House then postponed the debate to February 19.

On that date, Representative James Holland of North Carolina stated that he could see nothing wrong with foreigners; in fact, some of his best constituents were foreigners. Back home in North Carolina the Moravians had done no harm. But Mr. Holland's and Mr. Smilie's confidence in foreigners was not enough to prevent an amendment to the bill the next day asking six per cent interest on the whole of the last six payments after four years had passed. With the nation's financial interests thus safeguarded, a final vote was called for. There were forty-six yeas and forty-six nays. Speaker Nathaniel Macon, like Mr. Holland, was a North Carolinian, but apparently there were not so many Moravians among his constituents as there were among Mr. Holland's; he broke the tie by voting nay; the bill was lost; and the Harmonists' move to Indiana was delayed for eight years.

The second event of this early period suggesting that Harmonie was not altogether a happy community was of local importance only; but it was equally portentous, foreshadowing the difficulties that were to plague the society for many years, even after they did move to Indiana. These were difficulties created not only by native Americans, who could not understand the Württembergers, but also by fellow Germans, who could, and by themselves as well.

At the June session of the Court of General Quarter Sessions in Butler County, in 1809, one Jacob Schaal was indicted for libel against George Rapp. According to the report of the court's clerk, Schaal was accused of "publishing a false scandalous and malicious writing of and concerning the said George Rapp in the German language the meaning of which when translated is as follows:—'when you was in Philadelphia you did ramble with a whore and at the same time caused a miscarriage of the embryo by quick lime and white oil.' " This "writing" had been posted by the defendant in taverns and public houses.

In the end, Jacob Schaal was convicted, fined forty dollars, and warned by the court to keep a civil tongue in his head thereafter. The conviction is proof enough that George Rapp was not guilty of the "rambling" attributed to him. The significance of the trial, however, lies not in its outcome or even in the libel itself, but in the fact that a German-speaking citizen of that alien and unfriendly frontier land would hate a fellow-German violently enough to tell lies about him and that the Harmonists themselves would be sufficiently disturbed by the falsehoods of such a man to hale him into court. Suspicion and often envy among fellow-Germans as well as native Americans outside the Harmonist community, plus the Harmonists' own irrepressible inclination to go to court at every opportunity gave the Harmony Society a stormy history to the end of its days.

3

In 1807, "a fresh revival of religion" moved the Harmonists to adopt the custom of celibacy, which they practiced throughout the rest of their history. In later years, when Jonathan Lenz was a trustee of the society, he recalled that the custom originated among the young people, but Lenz was a babe in swaddling clothes in 1807 and could have derived this recollection only from hearsay.

Wherever the custom originated, the idea appealed strongly to the elders, and Father Rapp lost no time in finding Biblical endorsement of it in I Corinthians, 7:32-33: *He that is un-*

*married careth for the things that belong to the Lord, how he
may please the Lord: But he that is married careth for the
things that are of the world, how he may please his wife.*

He that is unmarried, Rapp reasoned, would therefore be a
better Harmonist. In a society where there was no privately
owned property or privately employed servant to covet, it was
best to eliminate wives too, or at least that function of wives
that is most frequently coveted. With that function eliminated
from a man's life he would no longer put family interests ahead
of community interests. Moreover, he would no longer be distracted from his daily work by the demands of the flesh, nor
would he further increase the burden of the community by producing children. As for woman in a sexless world, she would no
longer lose time from her communal labors in pregnancies,
childbirth, and the care of children, and she would cease wast-
ing precious hours prettying herself and flirting.

These were probably not the corollaries of the aphorism in
I Corinthians that St. Paul had in mind. At least, it would
seem from the rest of his meditations on the subject that he
was thinking of continence as a private and not a public virtue. St. Paul merely wished that everybody had as little trouble
as he had with the problem of sex and would "abide" as he did.
He was quite ready to admit that for those who could not
"contain" it was better to marry than to burn. Rapp, however,
saw a practical significance for his community in St. Paul's
mode of life, and as for the burning, he could only hope that
the increase of physical labor resulting from celibacy would reduce that discomfort to a minimum.

But Rapp's thinking was not based solely upon practical
concerns. He found that the rule of celibacy fitted neatly into
the whole structure of his theology. Just as justification for community of goods was obvious to him in The Acts 4:32, so a
close scrutiny of the Book of Genesis led him to the conclusion

that celibacy was a proper preparation for the millennium as well as a sound economic measure in a society like his.

For a long time, Rapp had believed that in the first days after the Creation Adam contained both sexes within himself and that originally there had been no need of woman at all. The twenty-sixth and twenty-seventh verses of the first chapter of Genesis read: *And God said, Let us make man in our image, after our likeness: and let them have dominion. . . . So God created man in his own image, in the image of God created he him; male and female created he them.* Rapp interpreted the plural *them* in these verses referring to Adam alone as the sexual duality in Adam before the female element was separated from him in the form of Eve, a separation that did not take place until the following chapter of Genesis.

When that separation did take place, Rapp decided, it was not a capricious act of God, nor was it an acknowledgment by God that He had made a mistake; it was, instead, a punishment of Adam for not being content with his original state. Adam had been restless and too preoccupied with the female element within himself, and when God finally observed that *It is not good that the man should be alone,* God was making an observation about Adam's behavior; He was not expressing an unfavorable opinion of His own handiwork.

Hoping to divert Adam from his preoccupation with himself, God created the beasts of the field and the fowls of the air and paraded them before Adam for Adam to name them. But Adam was diverted in the wrong way; he noted that their male and female elements were in separate bodies and he developed an irregular desire to be like them. This desire became so violent within Adam that it finally exhausted him and he fell into a deep sleep. Then came God's punishment; He took out one of Adam's ribs and created Eve.

When Adam awoke, he was no longer bisexual; he was a

mere male, and consequently slower witted about sexual matters than he had been previously. Eve, on the other hand, was more precocious about sex than Adam, since sex was the sole purpose of her creation. Encouraged by the serpent, she was soon offering Adam the fruit of the tree of knowledge of good and evil. Although God had forbidden him to eat this fruit, Adam tasted it, and at once he recognized what he had both lost and gained.

George Rapp believed the tree's fruit contained not only the poison of disease and death, which Adam would never have experienced if he had not eaten it, but also the seed of sexual passion, which is often described metaphorically as a fever culminating in a little death. At any rate, the son that Adam begat thereafter was *in his own likeness* and not *in the likeness of God,* like Adam himself. God's original plan therefore, Rapp reasoned, must have been a mingling of the male and female elements within Adam and creation of a new human being from Adam alone, without the pain of childbirth. Such an offspring would then have been the son of God, as Christ was to be later, and not the son of man.

Pursuing this interpretation further, Rapp discovered that many other events and statements in the Bible fitted into it. The immaculate conception of Christ, for example, became inevitable if Christ was to be a perfect man, representing once more the original plan that God had devised for a world without corruption and death. Rapp noted that after the first resurrection, according to Matthew 22:30, the risen saints would neither marry nor be given in marriage, as are *the angels of God in heaven;* and thus the circle would be complete.

From these interpretations George Rapp concluded that a celibate life would better prepare a man for acceptance in God's sight on the Day of Judgment. As for the future of a society waiting for the millennium with no progeny in prospect, he felt no concern, since he was convinced the millennium would come in his own lifetime. Anyhow, he believed that a prolonged practice of celibacy would restore man's ability to multiply himself alone, according to God's original plan for Adam.

The celibacy that the Harmonists imposed upon themselves applied to those who were already married as well as the unmarried. Men and women in wedlock continued to live together but were expected to abstain from further sexual relationship. Some failed in the endeavor. In the next twenty years, the Ralls, the Schwartzes, the Vogts, and the Killingers produced about two dozen children. George Rapp's own granddaughter, Gertrude, eloped in her youth with one of her tutors, but was persuaded by a friend to return to the community.

Offenders against the custom were not punished, although the patriarchal and communal disapproval must have been hard to bear. On one occasion, after the Harmonists moved to Indiana, Martin Rall went to Father Rapp for permission to build an addition to his house, and Rapp allowed him to use community lumber for the project, although he would not permit other members of the society to help with the job. Rapp reproved him, however, by saying, "If you would stop adding to your family, Brother Martin, you would have no need to add to your house." Some Harmonists, when they could no longer endure the burning of sexual desire, ran away or withdrew from the community formally. But, in general, disharmony decreased in Harmonie after the ban on sex, in direct contradiction to the cynical observation of Lord Byron in *Don Juan:*

> "Why called he 'Harmony' a state sans wedlock?
> Now there I've got the preacher at a deadlock.
> Because he either meant to sneer at harmony
> Or marriage, by divorcing them thus oddly.
> But whether Reverend Rapp learned this in Germany
> Or no, 'tis said this sect is rich and godly."

Rich the Harmonists did become in a very short time, and godly they remained, for the most part, according to the new rule of self-denial that they had set for themselves. In 1866, Aaron Williams was able to say, in *The Harmony Society at Economy, Pennsylvania,* "No children have been born in many years." And this in spite of the fact that new members still within the age of childbearing had joined the society.

After the Harmonists accepted the celibate state, their religious usages, other than the sacrament of marriage, remained the same. They abstained from unnecessary labor on the Sabbath and assembled twice on that day for worship, which consisted of prayers, the singing of hymns, and sermons by Father Rapp. Sunday evening was less holy than the rest of the day and was an occasion for band concerts. In addition to the observance of the Sabbath and the celebration of Christmas, Good Friday, and Easter, there were three annual Harmonist festivals that were of a religious or semireligious nature: the anniversary of the founding of the society (February 15); the Harvest Home (early autumn); and the Love Feast and Lord's Supper (late October). Punishment for violation of the communal laws, which were semisacred, was general ostracism by the community and public reproof. Funerals were simple, relatives and friends gathering in the house of the deceased and, after brief appropriate remarks, following the hearse to the community orchard, where the body was buried in a plain hexagonal box in a grave that was left unmounded and unmarked. Every night of the year, members of the society were reminded of their mortality as they kept watch by turns, when, after the crying of each hour, they added: "Another day is past and a step made nearer to our end; our time runs away, and the joys of heaven are our reward.'

In 1812, a death occurred in Harmonie, Pennsylvania, that has ever since been associated with the Harmonist rule of celibacy. It was John Rapp, aged twenty-eight, George Rapp's only son, who died, on July 27th, and soon thereafter gossip was abroad that he had succumbed under his father's knife while being castrated as punishment for sexual indulgence. Since this gossip has persisted virulently for a hundred and fifty years, it can not be ignored in any consideration of the New Harmony story.

When the Duke of Saxe-Weimar Eisenach was told the story in New Harmony, Indiana, in 1825, he said that he had already heard it in Germany before he left home. Later, the *Philadelphia North American* and the *Pittsburgh Gazette* engaged in a controversy over the scandal, perhaps inspired as much by the geographical rivalry between eastern and western Pennsylvania as by a quest for truth, since Philadelphians in those days delighted in proving that Pittsburghers were barbarians and Pittsburghers were prickly about their younger culture. In 1866, *The Atlantic Monthly,* sedate and proper as it was, stooped to the publication of a short story by an anonymous author who repeated the gossip, confusedly describing the victim as George Rapp's "brother" and calling him "Frederick." A few years later, an article in *Scribner's* kept the story alive by calling it "a cruel fiction." A lengthy history of Posey County, Indiana, printed in Chicago in 1886, preserved it locally by saying that "the story that John Rapp suffered a nameless punishment even unto death, at the hands of his father, is most bitterly denied by the society." Today everyone who knows anything about the Harmonists—and almost anyone who has visited in New Harmony, Indiana—has heard the story; and any conversation about the community, if it lasts long enough, leads eventually to someone's beginning a question with, "Do you think it's true that Father Rapp. . . . ?"

Such answers to this question as have been forthcoming from those who have written about the Harmonists have been varied and mostly vague. In widely dissimilar books about the society in Pennsylvania, both John Archibald Bole and The

Federal Writers' Project have been discreetly silent on the subject. In *The Harmonists: A Personal History,* John S. Duss, one of the last trustees of the Harmony Society, dismisses the tale in one sentence as "fantastic." Christiana F. Knoedler's *The Harmony Society* reports that George Rapp performed the marriage ceremony of his son John and that John's daughter, Gertrude, was born in 1808 (the year following the adoption of celibacy), and then goes on to say, with no discernible intention of humor, that in 1812 "the young man died of a serious accident." George B. Lockwood, in *The New Harmony Movement,* confuses John and Frederick Rapp, gets the date of death wrong, and then concludes that "a more probable story is that he was fatally injured by a falling tree." Marguerite Young, whose *Angel in the Forest* is subtitled "A Fairy Tale of Two Utopias," is both clinically and historically inaccurate in her reference to the story. "There was just a little trickle of blood," says she, "and then there was a dead body. It is a tale told in all the taverns, both in America and Germany. . . . Nothing has ever been said as to the fate of the widow, whether her skull and palms were cast upon the turnip fields, or what became of her." (The widow lived out her days in the Rapp household, dying March 8, 1873, at the age of eighty-five. Duss says her maiden name was Jacobina Diehm, but the Harmonist records at Old Economy call her Johanna.) Most specific of all historians is Aaron Williams, who wrote in 1866: "Mr. Baker, present head of the Society, was at work with young Rapp elevating grain in the Society's store, when Rapp strained himself, injuring his breast. After his death, he was dissected and water was found in his chest and one lung was destroyed." Williams claimed corroboration of this account from members who had left the community and who, he said, had no motives for disguising the truth.

Three facts surround with a certain degree of mystery the

relationship of John Rapp to his family and to the rest of the community.

The first is the absence of his signature from "The Articles of Association 1805." John Rapp, twenty-one years old in 1805, had played an active role in choosing the site for the community and in surveying it and preparing it for the arrival of his father's flock from Philadelphia. This important document bears the signatures of his father and his mother and even of his sister, Rosina, who was only nineteen at that time. One attempt to explain the missing signature has arisen from a conjecture that the contract of 1805 was not actually drawn up until several years after John's death and was then antedated by George Rapp's canny associates when it became advisable for them to have their social agreement in writing. This is a beguiling speculation, but it seems to be invalidated by the fact that the Articles of 1805 were signed by other members of the society who died soon thereafter and who consequently would not have been on hand to attach their signatures to the belated document. Among these signers was one Christopher Viehmeir, who was drowned in Connoquenessing Creek, according to a coroner's inquest of September 11, 1807.

A second curious fact is that in Gertrude Rapp's many sprightly letters she makes no mention of her mother, Johanna, who lived in the Rapp household. Gertrude was an affectionate and sentimental girl and wrote with warmth about her Grandfather (George Rapp), her Grandmother, and her Aunt Rosina; but her mother, John Rapp's widow, is omitted from all her comments on the family's life.

The third fact that sets John Rapp apart and can not be fully explained is that the only tombstone in the three Harmonist cemeteries—at Harmonie, Pennsylvania, at New Harmony, Indiana, and at Old Economy in Ambridge, Pennsylvania—bears John's name. It was donated to the community by "outside friends," but there is no explanation in Harmonist records or newspaper accounts as to why it was donated or, more important, why it was accepted and placed in the cemetery at Harmonie, Pennsylvania, in violation of the Harmonist practice of leaving graves unmounded and unmarked. For some reason, this tombstone does not stand over the grave itself but lies against the wall at the side of the cemetery, suggesting that the Harmonists accepted it from the donors reluctantly.

John Duss's translation of the German inscription on the tombstone reads as follows:

> *Here lies and rests in the cool bosom*
> *of the earth*
> *Johannes Rapp*
> *who*
> *was born the 19th of September 1783*
> *died the 27th of July 1812*
> *Here lies a clay upon the potter's wheel*
> *Until decay unlock*
> *The precious salt to a new body*
> *Which in the joy of life will then arise*

Was John Rapp a rebel, out of sympathy with his father's chiliastic dream, or was he merely absent on business on the day the Articles of Association 1805 were signed? Did his widow live in isolation in the Rapp household for sixty years after his death, ostracized by the family, never spoken to, never mentioned; or was there a basic antagonism between her and her daughter that made it impossible for Gertrude, affectionate though she was, to write warmly about her mother in her letters? Or was Johanna Rapp perhaps of unbalanced mind? If so, was it John's death that caused her to lose her reason? What special circumstances impelled "outside friends" to donate a marker for John Rapp's grave when no other Harmonist was ever so honored, not even Frederick Rapp or Father Rapp himself? Why did the Harmonists feel compelled to accept the gift in violation of their practices? And after they accepted it, why did they neglect to set it over the grave? Were the "outside friends" moved by sympathy for the Harmonists because of the ugly slander that had spread concerning the young man's death? Or was it John himself they were thinking of? Did they believe the accusations they heard? Did the Harmonists accept the unwanted gift because of shame or simple embarrassment? Any answers to these questions now can be only conjectures, just as conclusions about the nature of John's death at this late date can be only speculations.

It is not altogether inconceivable that George Rapp castrated his son. Castration was not an uncommon operation in the early 1800's. It was often prescribed in the treatment of mumps and other diseases, and for a time it was on the statute books of Pennsylvania as a punishment for sexual excesses. George Rapp had studied the nineteenth chapter of Matthew, drawing from it a conviction that redemption was not the result of sudden divine revelation but of a long slow process of recovery from original sin, and it is possible that the twelfth verse of this chapter persuaded him that this not uncommon operation of his day could also be a holy rite.

For there are some eunuchs, which were so born from their mother's womb: and there are some eunuchs, which were made eunuchs of men: and there be eunuchs, which have made themselves eunuchs for the kingdom of heaven's sake.

George Rapp might indeed have been so carried away by anger and religious ecstasy that he was willing to sacrifice the virility of his only son as an example to his people. Or young John himself, having read the twelfth verse of the nineteenth chapter of Matthew and despairing of ridding himself of his weakness, may have submitted willingly to the operation. Indeed, in a fit of contrition, he could have performed the operation on himself. Strange things are done by human beings to themselves as well as to others in the name of righteousness. Or perhaps John Rapp simply had mumps or ruptured himself "elevating grain in the Society store" and the operation was performed as therapy and afterwards the account of it and of his death was maliciously distorted by enemies of the Harmonists.

If the castration actually took place, this last explanation is the one that seems most likely when all the evidence is considered. The second-hand sources of the gossip, the malice and suspicion with which the Harmonists were already regarded in 1812 by many of their neighbors, and the viciousness of the canards that were spread about them, such as Jacob Schaal's tale of Father Rapp's "rambling," discredit the alleged castration as an act of vengeance or religious fanaticism.

Beneath the gentle and kindly quality of mind and heart that George Rapp professed in his letters there existed, it is true, a violent temper and a tyrannical nature; but even if there was, beneath these, a fanatic tendency toward sadism, he would certainly have been restrained by the counsel and the social pressure of the men around him. By 1812, George Rapp was not alone in his leadership of the Harmonists; he was still their spiritual leader, but constantly at his side now were his "associates," practical men aware of the commercial value of the Harmonist project. Even those who might have had something to gain from the removal of George Rapp's son would not have allowed Father Rapp to endanger such an investment by an act that would at best be described in court as manslaughter and in which they would themselves have a certain complicity. Finally, Aaron Williams, who accounts for John's death more specifically than any other historian, was a deliberate, devout, and conscientious man who would have found it morally impossible to condone or cover up an act that he could only have abhorred. Lively myth too easily persists in history where the simple truth is only dull and unexceptional.

4

By 1813, the Harmonists were enjoying a degree of financial success in Pennsylvania that would have satisfied most men. Their self-denial and their zeal had created harmony in fact as well as name, and by their perseverance and industry they had brought money pouring into the community till.

But the leaders of the Harmonists were not satisfied. They saw many disadvantages in the location they had chosen. For one thing, the distance of their town from the river—twelve miles—had to be covered by slow and expensive overland hauls before their goods were truly on their way to distant markets. For another, Pennsylvania's climate did not suit them. As they had said in their memorial to Thomas Jefferson seven years before, the land was "too brocken & too cold for to raise Vine." Finally, the seven thousand acres they had now acquired were insufficient for their purposes, cabining their dreams and confining their energies.

This last limitation set the Harmonist leaders to worrying about the future. There was little possibility of further expansion in the Connoquenessing Creek neighborhood. Owners of the land surrounding them were reluctant to sell and, when they did sell, sold dear, capitalizing upon the need of the Harmonists and the jealousy, suspicion, and animosity with which they were generally regarded. But without expansion and increase of labor members of the Harmonist Society would soon be enjoying more leisure than was good for them. Leisure would lead to idleness and idleness would quickly tempt Satan into their midst. What George Rapp and his associates wanted was a home for their people larger than Harmonie, Pennsylvania, at once more remote from gossiping neighbors and closer to river tranportation, a place where the sun was hot and the summer season long, where the land was level and the soil rich; in other words, an Eden, where the Württembergers could live as they had lived in Germany and yet as George Rapp believed God expected them to live in preparation for the millennium, uncorrupted from within or from without. Rapp finally found this Eden on the banks of the Wabash in Indiana.

In the winter of 1813–1814, George Rapp traveled west by boat and on horseback with Peter Schreiber and John L. Baker to look for a new townsite. Ohio, a rolling countryside of luxuriant peach and apple orchards, farms, and small towns, was already too well cultivated and too thickly inhabited for their purposes, and they did not pause in their quest until they reached Louisville. But there they soon discovered that the best land in that region also was taken if not already settled. They had thought they were not interested in the territory north and west of Louisville because they believed the Indians of that country were too numerous and warlike; but when they learned that the Battle of Tippecanoe had removed the Indian menace in that region, the three men traveled on and made Vincennes the headquarters of their search.

Vincennes, a town on the Wabash River of about 3,000 people, still predominantly French, was already an old town by western standards in 1814, with almost a century of history behind it. Three flags had flown over its fort, and its territorial legislative hall had once been the seat of government for part of the Louisiana Purchase as well as the Indiana Territory. For ten years Vincennes had boasted a newspaper, *The Western Sun,* and for eight years it had been the home of a university. The year before Rapp's arrival, a brick courthouse had been constructed, and a few fine mansions already graced the town, among them William Henry Harrison's stately "Grouseland," built on a high bank above the river.

At Vincennes, Rapp and his companions studied all the available parcels of land recorded in the territorial land office and made expeditions along the Wabash and overland to Princeton, a half day's journey from the site they finally chose. They liked especially the area south of Vincennes, where George Rapp admired the groves of black locusts more than anything else he saw. To his countryman's eye the acacia, or locust, meant that the earth from which they grew to such magnificence was undoubtedly fertile.

"You will not believe what a rich and beautiful land is here," he wrote back to his people in Pennsylvania; and on February 8, 1814, while the tract he had chosen was still in the grip of winter, he wrote to Frederick that, although it looked miserable enough, he saw in it the possibility of great and beautiful plans. There was plenty of upland for pasturing sheep, well-watered with streams, and the meadows were as level as a floor and yet with grade enough for drainage. Even so, he told Frederick, a steam engine would be needed if they continued manufacturing.

John Baker too was impressed.

"The property is covered with heavy timber," he wrote, "comprising oaks, beeches, ash, three kinds of nut trees, three to four feet in diameter, with trunks fifty to sixty feet high,—excellent material for all kinds of cabinet work. Gum trees, hackberry, sycamore, persimmons, wild cherries, apples and plums, also wild grapes of enormous diameter and height, all of which bear fruit.

"There are also a number of maple and sugar trees, from which great quantities of sugar can be made in the spring. Sassafras trees from two to three feet in diameter and a kind of poplar; these have a very solid good wood for lumber, while in the lowlands there are very large cypress trees good for the work of the cooper and for shingles.

"The forest abounds in antlered deer, bear, wolves, ground-hogs, hares, wildcats, squirrels, snakes, and wild turkeys (the male bird of the species often weighing as much as twenty-five pounds). There are many kinds of birds besides."

These were practical men. They had no time to record the poetry of the "many kinds of birds besides"—bright flocks of parakeets, like green leaves of summer left behind in the winter woods, woodpeckers, nuthatches, and the crested red cardinal and slate-blue titmouse already tentatively whistling their first clear calls of spring. The redbud was not yet in flower when George Rapp and his companions were there, nor the spicebush and the pawpaws that grew in abundance beneath the tall oaks and poplars; but even if they had been adorned in their spring magic, these trees would probably have been reported only as undergrowth that must be chopped away. These men thought only of clearing and building and making.

What they saw was the land cleared and used, rich first and second bottoms with rolling hills and Indian mounds stretching away to the west and south, and they found it exactly suited to their needs. They would not build the new town on the first bottoms adjacent to the river, where cane stood higher than a horseman's head. They knew the danger of floods and also of the miasma arising from such land, which people in those days believed was poisonous and the cause of malaria. They would build the town on the higher second bottoms, and thus their new Harmonie would be the riverport that George Rapp and his associates wanted but would stand far enough away from the river so that the rowdy, half-horse, half-alligator men they had seen on the Ohio and the Wabash would seldom molest or disturb the quiet-loving Württembergers. In that spring of 1814, George Rapp made an initial purchase of 24,734 acres of this Indiana land for $61,050 and then sent John L. Baker back to Pennsylvania to fetch a hundred of his people to start building the new town.

Back in Pennsylvania, the departure of this advance working party caused Frederick Rapp several unforeseen difficulties that were almost disastrous. At once the Pennsylvania authorities leveled a fine against the society for the failure of the departing men to serve their time in the militia. While quarrels and litigation over the fine were in progress, the neighbors round Harmonie began to trample the unguarded fields and gardens of the departed Harmonists and broke into their empty houses. The situation got out of hand when the vandals added insult to injury by demanding that they be allowed to elect from their own midst a commandant for the community to restore order out of the chaos that they themselves had created.

In May, 1815, when a Mennonite named Abraham Ziegler from Lehigh County appeared in Harmonie and offered to buy its buildings and its 7,000 acres for $100,000, Frederick Rapp, at his wit's end, accepted and closed the deal at once, although the profit on the total investment in Harmonie came to only $8,000. "I did not ask for any payment down," he wrote to his adopted father, "because I do not see that we need it." After all, with the Indiana land purchased, the Harmony Society still had a surplus of $12,000 on deposit in a Pittsburgh bank.

Meantime, Baker and his one hundred men and women had loaded boats with sufficient goods to give them a start in the west and, in June, 1814, spent two weeks floating down the Ohio River to the mouth of the Wabash below Mt. Vernon, Indiana, known then as McFadden's Landing. From that point they worked the boats up the quieter Wabash to a bend just above the site of the new town. There they disembarked and, cutting a road through the heavy growth of cane in the first bottoms, camped their first night under a large oak at the center of what would soon be another Harmonie, the spot at the corner of Church and Main Streets in modern New Harmony where the Rapp-Maclure home still stands. The next day they set to work clearing the trees and vines that covered their property and began to build temporary sod huts and half-faced camps to sleep in.

That first summer in Indiana was hotter than any the Harmonists had ever experienced either in Germany or in Pennsylvania, and the clearing of land and draining of swamps nurtured vapors that made the air almost unbearably humid, so that it seemed even hotter than it was. It nurtured mosquitoes too, and soon an epidemic of malaria struck the workers, reducing the labor force by half. John Baker himself, a man famous in the community for his great strength and vigor, was laid low for a time. But with cooler weather in the fall the epidemic subsided and the workers began the task of building more substantial homes of logs and, finally, some of brick.

Having closed the sale of Harmonie, Pennsylvania, Frederick Rapp came out to Harmonie, Indiana Territory, in the early summer of 1815, and on July 7 of that year he was writing:

"After a pleasant voyage of fifteen days we arrived in good health. I found my father and all my friends well and satisfied with the change they had made. Finding the land excellent and beautiful. They have done immense work, already 125 acres in corn eight to ten feet high. Harvest began the last week in June. Wheat and rye proved very good. It appears that this country, in a few years, in regard to cultivation of small grain and commerce, will become one of the most important parts of the union. On the Fourth of July 150 persons came into our town, all living from six to twelve miles from us. The climate is somewhat warmer here than in Butler County, yet it is not so extraordinary hot as the people here think. The greatest heat is 95 degrees. A constant and pleasant zephyr from the west renders the air cool and moderates the heat here more so than in your country. The water is very good. Our vineyard and orchard grow wonderfully, and give hopes that this country is well calculated for them.

"Our machines lie motionless till Fall: we are all engaged in building houses and clearing land. Store goods are scarce and sell very well here; silver is plentiful in circulation, and might get quantity for eastern notes with several per cent premium. My father finds himself right well here and makes you his cheerful compliments. My sister Rosina is well and sends her respects."

This letter demonstrates the progress Frederick Rapp had made in the new language in ten years. It also suggests that he was already beginning to pick up the dialect of the new region to which he had moved. "My father finds himself right well and makes you his cheerful compliments" quaintly combines a common Middle Western way of speech and a Germanic construction.

Five months later, Frederick wrote to John Woods, an Englishman who had come to live in Albion, in the Illinois country, nearby:

"This country seems to be very suitable for raising wine, and we shall strive to provide the western world with this article in a few years, and so do not regret in any way the change we have made. . . . We have more opportunity here than we had in Pennsylvania, to make of a wild country, fertile fields and gardens of pleasure."

John Woods was especially impressed by the Harmonists' sheep, which they had turned loose to forage for the first year in the three or four hundred acres of cane that they had fenced in on the Illinois side of the river. Woods noted that western Americans had an aversion to mutton. In his travels in the new country he encountered backwoodsmen without game who had lived on a diet of nothing but cornmeal for weeks rather than eat one of their sheep. Although the Harmonists' sheep were mainly merinos, bred principally for wool, they had the European's taste for lamb and mutton. Another English traveler of this period, Morris Birkbeck, made a similar observation about the western American diet. At Cincinnati, he noted in his diary in 1817, that in Kentucky "even the negroes would no more eat mutton than they would horseflesh."

Good lamb is still difficult to obtain today in southern Indiana markets; mutton is almost unobtainable. Sheep are still raised principally for wool. The Württembergers failed to change western America's preference for pork and beef just as they failed to change the local taste in drink; Frederick Rapp's dream of providing the western world with wine was to come to naught.

Two months after Frederick Rapp wrote to John Woods, he was still pleased with the removal to Indiana, but the first blush of enthusiasm for the new neighbors, who had turned out in great numbers for the free beer at the Fourth of July celebration, had begun to fade. On February 2, 1816, he was writing:

"Our land is the best I have ever seen in America in quality and situation. It has all kinds of useful timber, abounds in fine springs, free stone for building purposes, clay for brick and excellent pottery. Six miles away on our land is good iron ore, where a furnace may be built. This will be in a few years the most flourishing country in the U. S., not only in agriculture but also in commerce and domestic manufacture. We enjoy on an average better health than in Pennsylvania. Many of us had the ague and fever last fall, but that may be attributed to the change of climate. Men of learning and good moral character are very desirable in this country, that the natives might be brought to better order through them."

Perhaps Congressman Smilie knew what he was talking about ten years earlier when he said American frontiersmen needed the Württembergers' fine moral example. Nevertheless, Frederick Rapp was already revealing in the new country the aloof self-righteousness that had got the Württembergers in trouble in Pennsylvania and that was going to get them in trouble again. That old serpent, which is the Devil and Satan, had no better ally than self-righteousness in the new Hoosier Zion, especially when free beer flowed on the Fourth of July.

5

In New Harmony's very slight growth in one hundred and fifty years, the street plan that the Harmonists laid out in 1814 has been extended only one block to the north and one to the west and not many more than that in the other two directions. The two principal streets of Harmonist times—Main and Church—remain the principal streets of the village today, and the intersection of Main and Church, where the Württembergers camped their first night and where George Rapp later built his home is still the busiest intersection of the town.

As they had done in Pennsylvania, the Harmonists laid out their new Harmonie in the shape of a square, with the broad streets running at right angles according to the cardinal points of the compass. Along these streets they planted Lombardy poplars, which Frederick Rapp believed were a specific against malarial fever, but afterwards, when these trees proved short-lived in the sandy soil, they replaced them with mulberries. In all the residential areas there were public ovens and public wells at convenient intervals. Between the sidewalks and the streets they planted beds of flowers and useful herbs.

Main Street, running north and south, lies one block east of the original western boundary. At its southern end it becomes the road to Mt. Vernon. Here the Harmonists designed and planted a labyrinth, a circle of about one hundred and forty feet in diameter with deceptive twisting paths bordered by flowering hedgerows that led to a small temple in the center. The temple was thatched with straw and was rough and homely on the outside, but inside it was tiled and ornamented with religious symbols. The structure represented the beauty of a good man's spirit or soul contrasted with the ugliness of his body. In 1840 the hedges were cut down, but a hundred years later the whole maze was recreated as part of a state project that was underway to restore New Harmony.

At Main Street's northern end in Harmonist times, the street narrowed into a wagon road that crossed the first bottoms to a ferry and boat landing on the river. In 1824, William Pickering drew a map of Harmonie that recorded the distance from the intersection of Main and North Streets to the river as "nineteen chains and twenty-one links," or about four hundred yards. Today the road still exists, but the river has changed its course many times in the intervening years and the boat landing is no longer where it was. Every summer, at the point where the road begins, the lower bottoms become a moat of tall corn round the northern rim of the town, and often in winter and spring these bottoms are flooded. Modern New Harmony's access to the Wabash and to the bridge that now crosses it into Illinois is an extension of Church Street beyond the old boundary, West Street.

Diagonally opposite Rapp's home, on Main Street, the Harmonists built the second of their four large community dormitories for the unmarried, each of which housed sixty to eighty people. These dormitories were known simply and practically as No. 1, No. 2, No. 3, and No. 4. Rapp's home was sometimes called "No. 5," although it was not a dormitory in Harmonist days. Old No. 2, across from Rapp's home, still stands and is open to the public as a museum. Also on Main Street were the Tavern, "a private house of entertainment," so designated to give the tavernkeeper the right to exclude un-desirable guests, the community tannery, the town store, the doctor's and apothecary's houses, and the hatter's and wagon-maker's shops. Of these buildings only the apothecary's house remains. The Tavern was destroyed by fire in 1908 and the others have been torn down in the course of the years.

Between Main and East Streets and running parallel to them is Brewery Street, which got its name from the establishment that once graced its northern extremity. Catty-corner from the brewery, as they say in New Harmony, at the intersection of Brewery and North Streets, was the second distillery that the Harmonists built, and nearby was their second large pig-gery. Brewery Street must have been a pungent neighborhood. Nevertheless, the Harmonists built their hospital on it, and there is no record of objections to the smells by the Bessons, Bentels, Eigners, Kurzes, and others who lived roundabout. Perhaps they thought themselves no worse off than the Veltes, Stahls, and Boringers who lived at the other end of the street and who had to put up with a limehouse, a sheepfold, and a dye works. The "watch house" too was at the southern end of Brewery Street. Since this was an industrial district, the "watch house" was probably a clockmaking establishment and not a guardhouse, as its name implies. Harmonist records do not explain.

As already noted, Church Street began at West Street in-stead of the river's shore in Harmonist days, and from West it ran eastward across Main and Brewery to East and eventually divided into the wagon roads leading to Evansville and to Princeton. The Evansville road is a good black-topped highway today, known as The Harmony Way; the other road is paved too, but in its dog-legged contortions through Poseyville and Cynthiana it is hardly navigable at speeds faster than those of the wagons and coaches of the early settlers.

On Church Street stood both the churches that the Harmonists built. Neither remains, but modern New Harmony's schoolhouse, on the site of the second church, is graced by the door and the doorway of the old church. This door is of cherrywood and has a stone lintel on which Frederick Rapp carved and gilded a rose. The lintel also bears the date 1822 and a reference to Micah 4:8, which reads in translation from the Lutheran version of the Bible: *And thou tower of Eden, the stronghold of the daughter of Zion, the golden rose shall come, the former dominion, the kingdom of the daughter of Jerusalem.*

Also on Church Street were the saddler's and cooper's shops, a greenhouse and a cider-and-wine press, both located just behind George Rapp's home, and the community dormitories No. 3 and No. 4. For many years after the Harmonists' departure No. 3 was a hotel and was called "The Tavern," the original tavern on Main Street becoming known as "The Yellow Tavern." No. 3 was torn down in the late 1940's after it had stood vacant and neglected too long for it to be restored. No. 4 remained a dormitory for the followers of Robert Owen after the Germans left. Later, it became a tenement house, its sixteen rooms occupied by sixteen families. After that, for sixty years, it was a theatre. Today, with the words "Opera House" still carved over its doorway, it is a business establishment.

Granary and Tavern Streets flank Church, Granary to the north and Tavern to the south. The Harmonist tavern, "The Yellow Tavern," stood at the northwest corner of Main and Tavern. Tavern Street was principally residential, except for the tavern and the Harmonist school nearby, where Dr. Johann Christoph Müller presided and also operated the community press. The schoolhouse was torn down in 1913. Granary Street too was largely a residential street, except for its dye house and the big brick-and-stone granary, which is more often called, inaccurately, "the old fort," in modern New Harmony.

Below Tavern Street and parallel to it lies Steam Mill

Street. Here stood dormitory No. 1, a cotton factory, a cutlery, a ropery, and a ropewalk, the long narrow shed where the ropemaker paced backward paying out strands of material for his wheel. One block below Steam Mill Street is South Street, a motley neighborhood in Harmonist days. In addition to its half-dozen homes were a wash house, a light leather tannery and soap factory, horse stables, a colt pasture, a goose meadow, and a deer park. At its western end South Street sloped off in a southwesterly direction through a field of sugar cane past the original piggery and distillery toward the Harmonist dam and water mill.

In this neighborhood lived the Vogts, one of the families who continued to have children after the celibacy rule was adopted, and it was to this neighborhood that fourteen-year-old Christina Vogt came from Philadelphia to join her five brothers and sisters in the spring of 1822. What were the feelings of an adolescent girl whose parents were obviously among the few who could not "abide," as St. Paul counseled, in a community where celibacy was the rule? The Harmonists left no records of what went on in the hearts and minds of individuals in their community, and we can only guess their private lives and thoughts. But we do know that this little girl arrived in Harmonie, Indiana, with terror in her heart.

Abishai Way, the Harmonists' agent at Pittsburgh, put her aboard the steamboat *General Presley Neville* under the special care of Captain Matthew Magee, whom he described as "very much a gentleman and a man of honor." First, however, Abishai Way gave the little girl two dollars to spend on her voyage and bought her a new bonnet. Afterwards, he was still so concerned about her that he wrote two letters to Frederick Rapp about her. In one of them he said: "You are no doubt aware of the prejudices entertained and the hostility evinced by the uninformed and lower classes of Germans and many others against your society for the discipline that governs it. This little girl before she left Philad.ª has heard flashood agravated against you, so much indeed do those misrepresentations haunt her mind that all we were able to say to the contrary is insufficient to give her confidence that she is not going into absolute slavery. It will require time and gentle treatment to reconcile her to the situation."

Nothing more is known of Christina Vogt, but surely, whether she received gentle treatment or not, she was not too old to find some comfort in the attractions that South Street offered to a child—its horse stables, its colt pasture, its goose meadow, and its deer park.

Indeed all the bordering streets of Harmonie promised adventure to the diminishing number of Harmonist children. Open country lay just beyond them. Behind the houses on West Street were, first, the community orchards and, then, the river. East Street had stables and vineyards and prune orchards and a cotton gin, with twenty miles of Indian mounds and forest between them and the next town. North Street had a pottery and shared with Brewery Street the brewery, the second piggery, and the second distillery, not so alluring to little girls perhaps but a paradise for small boys; and beyond North were the canebottoms and the wagon road to the river.

Perhaps the Martin Ralls, as unable to "abide" as the Vogts, lived on North Street by choice, for the sake of their children, and not because they were relegated to that least desirable of neighborhoods by Father Rapp as punishment for their connubial indulgences. After all, the swamp behind their house was soon drained by a ditch that the Harmonists dug through the center of the town, between Main and Brewery Streets.

6

Reversing the usual procedure, the Harmonists built their first log houses on the periphery of the town and moved in toward the center as they progressed in their community planning. Thus they did not have to tear down temporary housing in order to construct their permanent homes.

Their first public structure, of course, was a church. Finished in 1815, it was of frame construction, two-storied, with six arched windows on each side and two at the ends, which also had rounded windows in the gables. A twenty-by-twenty-foot belfry twenty feet tall crowned the east end of the church above the entrance, and above this belfry was a hexagonal clockroom with two clockfaces eight feet in diameter, one on the northeast side and one on the southeast. The clock struck the hours on a large bell and the quarter hours on a smaller bell, and the bell tones, it was said, could be heard at a distance of seven miles in the surrounding woods.

Having greater faith in the Lord than in their own machinery, the Harmonists made a large sundial, which was hung, in the beginning, on George Rapp's home and, later, on the south end of No. 2. This sundial still records the hours for the townspeople of New Harmony, whereas the church steeple and its clock were shattered by a bolt of lightning after a few years. The steeple was not equipped with lightning rods, like George Rapp's home. The Lord was expected to take care of his own, which should have included George Rapp as well as churches. But George Rapp was inordinately afraid of two things throughout his life—lightning and steam engines.

In 1822, the Harmonists built their second church on a plan

that George Rapp said he had conceived in a dream. Some said he told his people the plan was revealed to him by an angel. The church was of brick and shaped like a cross, the two-story transept and the two-story nave each a hundred and twenty feet long and the center of the church rising in a single story to an impressive height of twenty-eight feet. On top of this church was a large dome encircled by a railed balcony on which the Harmonist band played on Sunday evenings. (The last Harmonist church, built in Economy, Pennsylvania, and still in use by a Lutheran congregation of Ambridge, has a similar dome and balcony.) Inside the Indiana church, supporting the roof, were twenty-eight Doric columns of cherry, walnut, and sassafras forming arcades into each wing, four of them supporting the central roof. Each column was hand-turned and highly polished, made from a single stick of timber about six feet in diameter.

William Hebert, a traveler, who saw this church in the course of its erection, wrote of it: "I could scarcely imagine myself to be in the woods of Indiana, on the borders of the Wabash, while pacing the long resounding aisles and surveying the stately colonnades. . . . As if, however, the good Harmonians could not lose sight of a gainful utility in anything, the vaults of their new church are appropriated to the reception of stores of various kinds. In descending from the steeple of the old church [the first, frame church] . . . we perceived that the upper compartment of that building was also used as a store for grain, earthenware, cotton, &c."

The other of the two most imposing buildings in the Harmonists' new Harmonie was the granary, which could be used if necessary as a fort. This structure still stands. The first story is of rough stone, the two upper stories of brick. The walls, two feet thick, provided an excellent defense against weevils, the scourge of pioneer wheat growers. For fireproofing—that is, to keep the grain cool and prevent spontaneous combustion—the two lower floors of the granary were laid with tiles. The third-story floor, however, was of wood. Tiles also covered the hipped roof. They measured seven by twelve inches and had hooks on them that lapped over the lathing to keep them from sliding off. The three thick doorways of the granary were fastened with heavy locks and barred with heavy timbers.

Soon after the construction of this granary a rumor spread that a secret tunnel connected it with Father Rapp's home and that Rapp used the tunnel to persuade his people that he had a magic talent for appearing out of the earth. While his people were at work, the rumor went, Rapp would pop out of his tunnel and make unannounced inspection tours. The gossips who invented the rumor failed to explain how the Harmonist workmen who dug the tunnel were kept from knowing what they were doing or from talking about their work after it was done. Since no one has ever found this tunnel and George Rapp's home did not have a cellar, the tale seems to be another of the scandalous inventions with which the Württembergers' neighbors plagued them throughout their history.

In their numerous industries, the ingenious Harmonists availed themselves of various sources of power. Most singular and spectacular—indeed almost unique in that region in their day—were the steam engine that operated their cotton mill and, later, their steam threshing machine. Most conventional for that early time, of course, was the water power that turned "the four run of stones" in the flouring mill at the damsite and the water power that turned the mill beside Gresham Creek two miles southeast of town. This Gresham Creek mill pressed oil from nuts. From our modern point of view, more unusual than either of these sources of power was the large dog that walked a treadwheel on a platform twelve feet above the floor in the brewery, pumping water for the brew. Big as this dog was, he must have been spelled by another like him from time to time, for the Harmonist brewery produced five hundred gallons a day.

The Harmonists drank some of this beer themselves, and they drank wine too, although Father Rapp rationed both beverages from the storehouse at his home. One European traveler remarked that their wine was as good as any he had ever tasted in France; he was not, it should be added, a Frenchman. Harmonist whiskey was equally noted for its excellence, but whiskey they did not drink. What is more, they were reluctant to sell it to their rowdy neighbors in Indiana and shipped it, instead, to safely faraway places like Pittsburgh and New Orleans.

Simple hand power was employed to move the greenhouse behind Rapp's home, but the fact that the greenhouse was movable is worthy of note. This glasshouse, heated in winter by tinplate stoves, traveled on rollers set in grooved rails that were fastened to a platform twice the size of the superstructure. Thus the Harmonist gardeners were able to push the big greenhouse back and forth to cover plants and trees on frosty nights and during inclement weather, instead of shifting the plants and trees themselves back and forth. By this device, they were able to make fig, lemon, and orange trees flourish in Indiana, as Schoolcraft noted on his visit in 1821.

Ultimately, in addition to the four big dormitories, the factories, and the other commercial buildings, George Rapp's followers constructed about forty substantial two-storied houses of brick and frame. According to Don Blair, of New Harmony, who has made a careful and enlightening study of Harmonist architecture and engineering, twenty-four of these dwellings were still in existence in 1963. George Rapp's own house, however, which was the most pretentious of all, was partially destroyed by fire in 1844. When Schoolcraft saw it in 1821, he remarked that it was a house "rather distinguished for capaciousness than taste."

George Rapp

Rapp's home in Iptingen, Württemberg

Rapp's home in Harmonie, Indiana

Frame church at Harmonie, Indiana, in Welby's *A Visit to North America . . .* , 1821

A Harmonist house

North doorway of the Harmonists' brick church, now in the west wall of the New Harmony school building

(Indiana State Library)

(Indiana Historical Society Library)

'Human Footprints
in Limestone

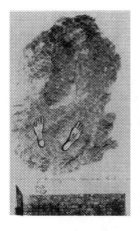
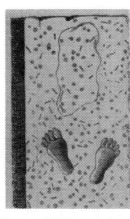
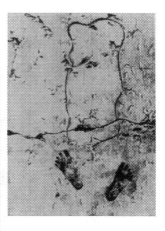

Drawings in Schoolcraft's article, June, 1822, and
in his 1825 book

Drawing in David Dale Owen's article, July, 1842

The footprints at the time of New Harmony's Centennial

A Harmonist wagon, built in 1823, and the Harmonists' fire engine, "the Pat Lyons"

Dormitory No. 2 with the sundial on the wall

Sundial of the Harmony Society

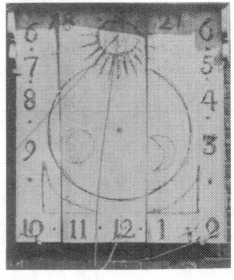

Rapp's house was a two-storied brick structure on a four-foot sandstone foundation set about thirty feet back from Church Street and Main Street at their intersection. A one-story ell at the west end was used as a kitchen. Verandahs bordered the south and east sides of the house, with flights of stone steps leading to the two entrances. After the fire of 1844, which was believed to have been of incendiarist origin, parts of the house were preserved as a nucleus for the Maclure mansion that was built on its site. The Maclure house, today owned by an Owen, still stands, but unfortunately a high brick wall now obscures its façade, which should be seen from some distance for its architectural beauty to be appreciated.

Although the Harmonists built their dwellings, both brick and frame, in a variety of arrangements, these houses were all prefabricated to a degree that was unique in a period long before men dreamed of mass production and standardization as methods of speeding construction. Each piece of lumber used in these houses was numbered with an adz and was of standard measurement. When a house was to be built, the builders made an inventory of the necessary parts and ordered them from the central storehouse. When, as seldom happened, repairs were required, the storehouse delivered by number the parts that were needed. The mortise and tenon joints that held these parts together were secured by pegs in round holes driven in so tight that an almost solid piece of wood was created out of the joint.

The Harmonists engineered their homes from the ground up with great foresight. They set flat stone footings in the earth well below the frost line and laid the footings of chimneys separately to allow for any difference that might occur in settling. In order to build fireplaces on more than one side of the chimney and thus make one chimney serve more than one room, they set chimneys off-center in the foundations of the houses, but not at the outside walls. In the attics they curved them to come out through the roof ridge, so that no leak-springing valley would be created between chimney and roof on any of the chimney's sides. Where stoves were used, the stovepipe was not bent to a flue in the chimney on the first floor but ran straight up through the ceiling and was widened on the second floor to a five-by-three-foot drum that served as a second stove without the need of a second fire.

The Harmonists built their homes for summer as well as winter weather and came about as close to the results of modern air conditioning as was possible for their times. They began in the cellar with a tunnel that ran from the outside wall to the floor and carried cool air down to force the hot air out of the cellar through a window on the opposite side. Above the cellar, they insulated the first-floor and second-floor ceilings with "Dutch biscuits," which were their own invention, slabs of wood wrapped in straw and mud and inserted in grooves between the ceilings and the floors. In addition, they insulated the sides of both brick and frame houses with loose, half-baked bricks, installed wet between the inside and outside walls. Interior dividing walls were insulated in the same way, making the rooms not only cool in summer and warm in winter but also soundproof.

Poplar and walnut were the the woods most frequently used in house construction, and because of their close tough grain they have remained almost completely impervious to termites and other insects through the years. Harmonist plaster and mortar were made of mussel shells from the Wabash River. Their plaster and mortar too have survived New Harmony's humid heat and cold, and the exterior brick work and the finish of interior walls have required few repairs.

That the houses were well cared for, once they were occupied, goes without saying; these people were Germans, and Germans are noted for careful housekeeping; they were also communists, and any damage to a home or neglect of it injured the neighbors as well as the occupants. John Duss reports, in his recollections of community life among the Harmonists, that a boy who scuffed his shoes was not only reprimanded by his parents but also condemned by his playmates, because he was damaging common property. A man who failed to keep his dwelling in proper condition was an even worse public offender.

The Harmonists always thoroughly cleaned their shoes before entering a house and took them off when they went upstairs. They never carried heavy furniture up the narrow flights of stairs for fear of chipping the plastered walls or scarring the woodwork; instead, they hoisted such objects through the floor above, where, along the side of each upstairs room, about two feet of the flooring was laid in such a way that it and the insulation could be removed for this purpose. Nor was furniture left on the floor to be marred by mops and brooms when the house was cleaned. On the walls there were racks where the women hung chairs and small tables at housecleaning time. The Harmonists, incidentally, created no distinctive type of furniture, but they exhibited excellent taste in purchasing most of their furniture from Shakers, whose craftsmanship was unrivaled in the area.

What the Harmonists built in their ten years in the Indiana wilderness is best summed up by the advertisement that Frederick Rapp finally wrote for the sale of the town on April 11, 1824:

"Town of Harmonie with 20,000 acres of first-rate land adjoining, situated on the east bank of the Big Wabash, seventy miles by water from its mouth, only fifteen miles by land from the Ohio River. Wabash is navigable at all seasons for boats of twenty tons burden, and a great part of the year for steamboats of middle class. Two thousand acres of highly cultivated land, fifteen of it in vineyard, thirty-five acres in apple orchard, containing 1,500 bearing apple and pear trees. Considerable peach orchard and pleasure gardens with bearing and ornamental trees.

"One large three-story water-powered merchant mill; extensive factory of cotton and woolen goods, 2 sawmills, 1 oil and hemp mill, 1 large brick and stone warehouse, 2 large granaries, 1 store, a large tavern, 6 large frame buildings used as mechanic's shops, 1 tanyard of fifty vats, 3 frame barns 50 x 100, with one thrashing machine; 3 large sheep stables, 6 two-story brick dwellings, 60 x 60; 40 two-story brick and frame dwellings; 86 log dwellings; all houses have stables and gardens; 2 large distilleries, 1 brewery."

7

The ten years they lived in Indiana were the Harmonists' halcyon years. They had some trouble with their neighbors, but nothing like what they had experienced in Pennsylvania. There was no violence. They never had to use their brick-and-stone granary as a fort.

Neighboring backwoodsmen came to the exotic little village on the Wabash, perhaps hoping for free beer, some of them ready to carouse if they could, but mostly just to stare—a not uncommon practice wherever the unfamiliar is on view; and some scratched and wagged their heads and some spat, and one is reported to have remarked, "I thinks and thinks about it." Some went away gossiping, since they were not sure just what was going on behind the scenes in Harmonie. But the gossip was never so diabolical as the story that was started in Pennsylvania about the death of Father Rapp's son, and there was no vandalism comparable to the invasion of vacated Harmonist property during the exodus for the west.

While the Harmonists were in Indiana, they had some internal difficulties, but again those difficulties were not so great as the disharmony that came before and after their residence in Indiana. In the ten years of their life on the Wabash there were only thirteen withdrawals from the society as against twenty-three in the nine previous years when they were living on Connoquenessing Creek, and no disorder assailed them like the disruption of their lives six years after they left the Wabash and returned to Pennsylvania when one Bernhard Müller, spuriously calling himself a count, came from Germany, corrupted the Harmonists to the point of a battle in their own quiet streets, and carried off two hundred and fifty of their number and a large portion of their capital to form a new community on the Red River in Louisiana.

In Harmonie, Indiana, the daily routine was peaceful and, except on Sundays and holidays, unvaried. Between five and six every weekday morning the silver tones of French horns wakened the members of the society to the day's work. Soon afterward the community milkwagon came along the streets, its wheels crunching in the gravel, the milkman's bell ringing, and to the sides of this wagon were fastened bulletins that notified individuals of special tasks for the day or dismissals from regular duties.

Maybe the grape harvest was coming in and more help was needed at the wine press. Maybe three men were excused from the day's plowing to assist Simon Durwachter with the building of his house on West Street. Maybe Jacob Wohlgemuth's fever was considered bad enough for him to be assigned to house-cleaning chores at No. 4 instead of heavy labor in the fields. Maybe Mrs. Rall or Mrs. Vogt was again in the throes of childbirth and a midwife was needed. These notices the Harmonists read while they poured in at the top of the wagon's tank the product of the previous evening's milking and drew off from the spigot at the bottom their own day's ration of milk.

After breakfast and the feeding of private flocks of chickens (the only creatures that refused to adapt to communism), the men—and, in busy seasons, the women with them—marched singing to the fields, where they worked till sunset. They paused at nine for lunch, at noon for dinner, at midafternoon for *vesperbrot*, and looked forward thereafter to the supper they would enjoy when they returned to the village.

As they worked or took their rest periods, the community band often played for them on a hillside nearby, or Father Rapp came out and watched them, exhorting them from time to time through his speaking trumpet. Those who worked in the factories and mills and shops were similarly visited by Father Rapp and the departmental superintendents and the band. These laborers sang when the work was not too heavy, and fresh-cut flowers often adorned their workbenches.

At nine o'clock, the curfew rang and the watchman began his nightly rounds. After that, the only Harmonists besides the watchman who were not in their homes and dormitories in bed were the herdsmen, who slept in the woods, in a house on wheels known in the community as "Noah's Ark."

Few visitors came to Harmonie, Indiana, who did not comment on the stillness of the village, for there was no roistering in the Tavern nor was there loitering in the streets. Each man and woman was busy at an assigned task, and idle conversation was not one of the arts they cultivated. The other aspects of the communists' life noted by visitors, most of them English travelers, were the regularity of their movements, their simple uniform dress, and their general good health.

On his third visit to Harmonie, on August 3, 1817, Morris Birkbeck observed: "It was (Sunday) evening when we arrived, and we saw no human creature about the streets:—we had even to call the landlord of the inn out of church to take charge of our horses. The cows were waiting round the little dwellings to supply the inhabitants with their evening meal. Soon the entire body of people, which is about seven hundred, poured out of the church, and exhibited so much health, and peace, and neatness in their persons, that we could not but exclaim."

The next year, 1818, Elias Pym Fordham was in Harmonie, reporting: "Their cooking, their dress, is exactly the same as it was on the banks of the Rhine. Their language is German. They are orderly, civil people, and their town is already very neat. The houses, log-built, are placed at regular distances, and are each surrounded by a neat kitchen and flower garden, paled in. The footpath is divided from the road by rows of lombardy poplars. M^r. Rapp's house is a handsome brick building, by far the best in Indiana.

"The Harmonists have, to each family, a cow, which comes to its owner's gate every morning and evening. In the woods they are kept by herdsmen. They have public ovens, public stores, and everything in common. They brew beer and make wine: the latter is kept for the sick and to sell. They all dress alike:—Mr. Rapp as the meanest laborer;—except when he goes out of town.

"They are great musicians, and many of them study music as a Science. Once a week they have a concert at Mr. Rapp's, to which I am invited.

"Their church is a neat wooden building, painted white. It has a tower, a bell, and a clock. The men sit at one end of the church and the women at the other; and Mr. Rapp sits while he preaches in a chair placed on a stage, about one yard high, with a table before him. When I heard him one weekday evening, he wore a linsey woolsey coat and a blue worsted nightcap. In praying the Harmonists do not rise up or kneel down, but bend their bodies forward, almost to their knees. Their singing is very good."

On November 21, 1819, came William Faux. His welcome was not so cordial as Fordham's had been, and he was soon disgruntled by a rebuff from the Harmonists. He had this to say:

"At Harmony till ten o'clock when we were told 'we must depart, or stay till after the morning service,' which commences at ten o'clock. At the moment the bells began chiming the people, one and all, from every quarter, hurry into their fine church like frighted doves to their windows . . . the males entering at the side, the females at the tower, and separately seated. Then enters the old High Priest, Mr. Rapp, of about eighty [he had just turned sixty], straight and active as his adopted son, Frederick, who walks behind him. The old man's wife and daughters [Rapp had only one daughter; the other women were probably his granddaughter, Gertrude, and his daughter-in-law, Johanna] enter the crowd, from his fine house, which looks as if the people who built it for him, thought nothing too good for him. . . . The women are intentionally disfigured and made as ugly as it is possible for art to make them, having their hair combed straight up behind and before, and a little skullcap, or black crape bandage, across the crown, and tied under their chin. . . . At present, the dwellings with the exception of Rapp's and the stores and the taverns, are all log houses. . . . They work very gently but constantly."

Two years later, on July 19, 1821, Henry Schoolcraft watched fifty to sixty women at noon march out to reap and bind oats. Each carried a long wooden rake and wore a large straw hat. Their dresses were of gray cotton cloth. "Of the personal attractions of females of this masculine species of labor," Schoolcraft remarked, "it is not necessary to speak."

When William Hebert was in Harmonie two years after Schoolcraft, in September, 1823, he found the Harmonists suffering from the fevers common to that time of year in that climate and in that era; but he too commented on the peace and order and the stillness of the town. In a remark about the absence of "the pursuits of literature" among the Harmonists, he was correct so far as the majority of them were concerned, but the village had a high rate of literacy and the people were informed about "the outside world." In their Indiana years, the Harmony Society subscribed to eleven newspapers, including *The Western Sun* of Vincennes and some Philadelphia and Louisville journals, owned a library of three hundred and sixty volumes, and offered for sale to the public in their community store Plutarch's *Lives*, *Pilgrim's Progress*, *The Vicar of Wakefield*, and other books.

Hebert also reports in his notes on the Harmonists that they had no printer "and seem fully persuaded that the employment of one, if it would not be detrimental to their peace or their interests, is at least superfluous to them." But within two months after Hebert's visit, Harmonie had both a printer and a printing press. Their versatile schoolmaster, Dr. John Christoph Müller, was at work in the schoolhouse on Tavern Street learning to set type in a flat-bed wooden press, from which the first results were proof pieces dated January 9, 1824.

Hebert's reactions to the Harmonists were mixed. He admired their material accomplishments, but their inability to speak the English language and their practice of celibacy seemed to offend him in about equal degree.

"These good people," he wrote, "have literally 'made the barren wilderness to smile' with corn fields, meadows, and gardens upon a most extensive scale. Their little town, seen from the neighboring hills, which are covered with their vineyards and orchards, has an exceedingly pleasing appearance, the Wabash, which is here an ample stream, being seen to wind its course in front of it, and beneath the luxuriant and lofty woods on the opposite bank of Illinois. . . . The log cabins are giving place as fast as possible to neat and commodious brick and frame houses, which are extremely well built, the uniform redness of the brick of which the majority of them is composed giving to the place a brightness of appearance which the towns of England are quite destitute of. . . . Amongst Indian woods which have but lately resounded with the yells of their untutored inhabitants, rises the pretty village church, the white steeple of which, seen from afar through the widely extended clearings and forests of girdled trees, seems to invite the traveler onward to a peaceful resting place. . . .

"As you may suppose, the utmost regularity and decorum subsists among them. . . . Their town is consequently very still, the sounds of mirth or conviviality being rarely heard within it, excepting when their American or English neighbors resort there for purposes of trade or to negotiate their money transactions. . . . These good people retain their German style of dress. There is nothing remarkable in that of the men. The women wear close and long-bodied jackets, or spencers, and gipsey bonnets. They are said to be a healthly looking people, and I imagine they are so, although this was not the case at the time of our visit, which was at the latter end of September, that being generally the most trying time of the year, and a considerable number of them were sick."

The Harmonists prospered in Indiana not only because of their industry and the regularity of their lives but also because the Indiana land was richer and more productive than the Butler County acreage and because access to markets via the western waterways was easier and more direct. Soon they had branch stores upriver in Vincennes and across the river in Shawneetown, Illinois, and agents represented them in Pittsburgh, St. Louis, and Louisville. By 1820, Frederick Rapp was reporting the annual value of their market goods as $50,000, and this in spite of the poor demand for their manufactured articles, especially woolens, which they had to price higher than imported cloth. Three years later, the Harmonists were able to offer the State of Indiana a loan at six per cent interest.

Their prosperity depended mainly upon their success in agriculture, which grew yearly in spite of a general depression prevalent in the western country in that period. In 1823, Jonathan Lenz, then only sixteen, took a flatboat to New Orleans with a cargo valued at $1,369. It consisted of thirty-nine kegs of lard, one hundred kegs of butter, six hundred and eighty bushels of oats, eighty-eight barrels of flour, one hundred and three barrels of pork, thirty-two oxen, sixteen hogs, and forty barrels of whiskey; and young Jonathan was only one of many who went South with boats so laden with Harmonist goods. In New Orleans, the flatboats were broken up and the lumber sold, the flatboatmen returning on foot or horseback over the Natchez Trace, or, if George Rapp and his associates happened to be feeling generous, via steamboat.

The year before Lenz's journey, in October, 1822, the Corydon (Indiana) *Gazette* published a report on the Harmonist Society written by a correspondent who signed himself "Oracle."

"Harmonie, Ind. A correspondent who resides at or near this place has occasionally informed us of the progress of this singular society under the direction of Mr. Rapp who appears to possess extraordinary power, as the civil and ecclesiastical ruler of the famous community. The letter now before us states, that for about six years the married women have not had any children, and that among many handsome girls and fine young men an astonishing degree of obedience to (supposed) orders has been observed. This society removed from Pennsylvania a few years ago—they now have a handsome town in Indiana, adorned with a splendid church having an elegant steeple, and other public buildings—though generally, all in common. It appears that they honored the last anniversary of American independence and furnished a free dinner and plenty of beer to all who pleased to visit them, treating them, also to fine music from their band. The writer goes on to state that besides the great quantities of grain and other vegetables, beef, pork, &c. that they raise, the amount of their manufacuring industry may be estimated as follows:

"Hatters and shoemakers, value per day	$30
Distillers and brewers	30
Spinning and carding	15
Blacksmithing and coopers	15
Various cloths (cotton)	25
—do— (woolen)	70
Flannels and lindsey	20
The tannery	15
Wagon makers and turners	12
Steam and other mills	15
Saddlers &c.	15
	$262

"Product of manufactures, 262 dollars per day, with a large value in agricultural products. We can not determine the correctness of the aggregate, but from what we know of the society, it is probably within the daily earnings of this laborious people. We must confess, however, that zealous to see as much as we can, the power of the republic in population and force, we can not approve the neglect of the first command in a 'legitimate' way."

The figures in this report were confirmed by *Niles' Weekly Register,* Hezekiah Niles's journal published in Baltimore.

The society continued to expand their holdings, buying land until the very year of their return to Pennsylvania. In 1819, they added 2,867 acres for the price of $7,318.64, and in 1824, the year of their departure, they bought 1,444 acres for $2,841.80. Some of this land they bought for speculation of course, reselling it in small parcels; some acreage they bought to protect themselves against the encroachment of undesirable neighbors. In 1817, when Posey County was enlarged to include all of Harmonie and there was a movement to change the county seat from the little settlement of Blackford to the Württembergers' town, the Harmonists contributed one hundred acres of land for the site of the new seat of county government at a place to be called Springfield, some ten miles away. The Harmonists had not become public-spirited, however; they simply did not want "foreign" English-speaking people coming to their village to conduct the county's business and they were willing to pay a price to preserve their isolation. Later, Mt. Vernon became the county seat, five days after the departure of the last contingent of Harmonists from Harmonie in 1825.

The town of Harmonie was not originally established in Posey County, but in Warrick County. Posey was not formed until November 1, 1814, some five months after John L. Baker disembarked his one hundred town-builders from their flatboat on the Wabash. The northern boundary of the newly created Posey County was set on a line known as Rector's Base Line, and this line cut through the village the Harmonists were laying out. For several years those Harmonists who lived south of Church Street were residents of Posey County and those whose homes were north of Church inhabited Gibson County. These Gibson County homes included the Rapp family mansion, and that is why Frederick Rapp, when he was elected to Indiana's Constitutional Convention in the spring of 1816, went to the territorial capital, Corydon, as a delegate from Gibson, and not from Posey where most of his people lived.

8

Frederick Rapp's duties as a delegate to the Constitutional Convention began at Corydon on June 10, 1816, and his first task in that overcrowded little town, which William Henry Harrison had named for the hero of his favorite song in the *Missouri Harmony* songbook, was to fight for his right to be there. The legality of the votes in the Harmony Society was challenged. Had the inhabitants strictly observed the Gibson-Posey line that divided their village? Had their votes been properly counted? Were they indeed entitled to vote at all? Or was this challenge in the opening session at Corydon simply a device on the part of the antislavery delegates to discredit the proslavery delegations from the western counties, of which Rapp was one? Because of the vagueness of the charges, the confusion of motives, and the difficulty of answering these questions, no action was taken and Rapp was seated.

Partisan histories of the Harmony Society never fail to point with pride to the fact that the Württembergers' business manager was a delegate to Indiana's first Constitutional Convention, but none of them acknowledges the fact that his election by his well-disciplined community was a foregone conclusion and that during his three weeks in Corydon his principal endeavor appeared to be frustration of the Convention's activities. On the opening motion of the Convention, which declared that it was "expedient, at this time, to proceed to form a Constitution and a State Government," Frederick Rapp, aligning himself with seven of the forty-one voting delegates, voted *no*. In this vote, Rapp may have been influenced by an editorial in the Vincennes *Western Sun* that had argued against formation of a state government on the grounds that governmental expenses would be greatly increased; but one of Rapp's later votes in the Convention, on June 20, can hardly be interpreted as anything but a willingness to identify himself with the proslavery forces.

The antislavery delegates, who were in the majority, had drawn up an article that read: "But, as the holding of any part of the human creation in slavery, or involuntary servitude, can only originate in usurpation and tyranny, no alteration of this constitution shall ever take place so as to introduce slavery or involuntary servitude in this state, otherwise than for the punishment of crimes, whereof the party shall have been duly convicted." On June 20, John Johnson, a delegate from Knox County, who only the year before had handed down a judgment from the bench of the Territorial Supreme Court upholding the ownership of a slave in Vincennes, and who with Frederick Rapp had voted against the enabling motion that opened the Corydon convention, proposed an amendment to the antislavery article. Johnson moved to substitute for the direct statement that "no alteration of this constitution shall ever take place" the controversial words, "it is the opinion of this convention that no alteration of this constitution ought ever to take place." Johnson's amendment would thus have left the slavery issue open for future consideration in the state's history, and Frederick Rapp was one of the minority of seventeen delegates who voted in favor of weakening the constitution in this way.

However, when the constitution was finally completed and Indiana came in free, Frederick Rapp was among the signers. The signing of the document took place on June 29, 1816. Four years later, Frederick Rapp was one of eight commissioners appointed by the Indiana Legislature to choose the site of a permanent capital.

The conclusion to be drawn from Frederick Rapp's record at the Constitutional Convention of 1816 and his subsequent recognition by the State Legislature is that, while he was a man not much moved by principle in public affairs, he had a strong sense of expediency and a good measure of common sense. Principles were hardly involved in the selecting of a site for a state capital; common sense was a more desirable virtue than idealism in such an action. Rapp's practical common sense was in part responsible for choosing almost at the center of the state an uninhabited, nondescript, and hence uncontroversial parcel of land that has since become the city of Indianapolis.

Before coming to America, George Rapp had preferred a free

state to a slave state for his experiment in religious communism, and there can be no doubt that Frederick Rapp shared the older man's preference, if only for practical considerations. Negro slavery in the vicinity of the Harmonist experiment would have undermined the leaders' discipline and damaged the community's economy. Harmonists would have asked themselves, "Are we any better than slaves?" and their German labor, with a high standard of living, would have had to compete with slave labor. What Frederick Rapp shared with Father Rapp was apparently no more than a practical preference for freedom. In the light of his actions at Corydon, it could not be called a moral principle, or, if it was, he was quite ready to compromise it. At Corydon, when he balanced the possibility of increased taxation and stricter governmental control of the Harmonists' investment on the Wabash against the issue of slavery, he voted with the proslavery forces.

Here was one of the sources of the animosity the Harmonists inspired among their neighbors wherever they went. The isolation they imposed upon themselves by refusing to learn the language of their adopted country, by clinging to the customs and the dress of the Vaterland, and by the vagueness and mystery of their religion and their exotic communal practices was aggravated to the point of ostracism and enmity by their self-centered and thoroughly materialistic conduct of relations with the outside world. They not only refused to be assimilated, they refused to share with any degree of altruism the responsibilities of citizenship in their adopted land.

For example, after Indiana became a state, a law was passed assessing a fine of seventy-five cents a day for every day's absence from the annual period of militia duty required of all able-bodied men between the ages of eighteen and fifty. Frederick Rapp carried on an energetic battle with the state over these fines and finally succeeded in having them reduced for the Harmony Society. This victory could hardly have endeared the Harmonists to those around them who were not so well organized politically as the Württembergers. Pacifism was always suspect among the pioneers of course, as witness the difficulties the Society of Friends encountered, but special economic privilege seemed to the pioneers inexcusable.

When dealing with individuals, Frederick Rapp was equally sharp with a dollar, even when dealing with friends. Morris Birkbeck, one of his best customers, who was a partner of George Flower in Illinois and who had high praise for the Württembergers on his early visits to the community across the Wabash, learned this harsh fact about Frederick Rapp the hard way. Rapp once cashed two drafts for Birkbeck on foreign exchange for $2,150, as one of his many legitimate money-making procedures; but when the drafts were returned with protests, he handed Birkbeck a bill for over four hundred dollars, basing his claim for the money on an obscure statute that entitled him to "20 per cent damages on the principal of the protested bills beside the interest from the date the bills were made until paid." It is significant that John Duss, who was raised in the Harmonist discipline, makes note of this financial coup of Frederick's with undisguised glee in his history of the Harmonists; and it is not at all surprising that in all of Birkbeck's subsequent comments on the Harmonists he was never again quite convinced that their leaders were sincere.

From the beginning the Harmonists had been relentless in their pursuit of the dollar, and whenever they were thwarted in that pursuit they became litigious. The records of their early dealings in Pennsylvania are full of recriminations and complaints. "I am determined to be played the fool with no longer," wrote one John Layer to George Rapp from Greensburg, Pennsylvania, in 1808, "—and I will have what's justly coming to me if there is Law and Justice in the country." In 1809, Jacob Neply of Jefferson County, Ohio, became so incensed in a wrangle over some grape plants stolen from his vineyards by a member of the Harmony Society that he wrote in a postscript to one of his letters:

"In the Name of the Lord God Amen

"Now father Rapp is it posiple you woold receive such goods knowingly as them grape plants that Jacob Willhoff brouht to you = And is it Posible you will keep a man one day in your society without making Restoration to the injured. Now lay your hand to your heart = Do not let us go farther to law. Willhoff hath introdust leaven enough into your Sosiety to sour the whole lump, if that leaven is not purge out I must conclude the whole lump is impure."

From "Pirmont Farm" at Connellsville, Pennsylvania, one Polly Rogers wrote pathetically to Frederick Rapp on December 14, 1812:

"Sir I have sat down to address you on a subject witch i am much interested the bargin that mi brother made with you when you was at mi father's was an entire secret to the familey untill his return from Pittsburgh mi father is not pleased with it he think it entirely too small a some for so large a flock of sheep

"Do Mr. Rapp consult your concious and see if it dont tell you so mi brother has been setting and mooping in the corner ever since I dont no from wat it arises if it is not from parting with his sheep

"I do believe in mi own mind he does rue it for mi part i do for my brother has allways bean raising mi vanity with making a fortune for me by the sheep but I think i am now disapounted tho I have so good an opinion of your goodness that I think you will compensat me for it yet

"now Mr. Rapp take it into consideration and I no you will say yourself that you have got these sheep for less than half their value I supos you will think that I mak mi self very buisy but I am very much interested on the subject

"no more at present But I want you to write very soon I wish to heare from you"

No record reveals whether Polly Rogers ever heard from Frederick Rapp, but certainly her irate father and her "mooping" brother would have found it hard, in any event, to think well of a man who did not consult his "concious" before he made such a deal as he had apparently made with the boy in Mr. Rogers' absence.

The year after Frederick Rapp's services as a delegate to the Constitutional Convention at Corydon, one hundred and thirty new members came from Germany to join the Indiana community, bringing the total population of the town on the Wabash to about eight hundred. The next year the morale of the society was so high that its members made two further sacrifices to what they considered their common welfare. One was the abolition of the use of tobacco. The other, made at the suggestion of Father Rapp, was the burning of the book that contained the list of contributions from members to the common stock of the society.

In this same year—1818—Morris Birkbeck reported that the Harmonists were planning to build a steamboat, "as a regular trader, to carry off the surplus produce, and bring back coffee, sugar, and other groceries, as well as European manufactures." This dream was never realized, however; at least, not on the banks of the Wabash. The next year was the year of the purchase of 2,867 additional acres, and the year following was the year the community was honored by the appointment of Frederick Rapp to the commission that chose Indianapolis as the capital of the state.

In 1821, a contract for the new members from Germany was

drawn up and signed (*see Appendix B*). This second Harmonist contract was bolder and more binding than the one that had established the society sixteen years before. The following year, 1822, the Harmonists' prosperity in Indiana reached its peak when John L. Baker and John Reichart went back to Germany and, in spite of many legal difficulties, which included unforeseen divorces and charges of desertion and assessments for unpaid taxes, collected 20,706 gulden in inheritances fallen to the members of the society and therewith fattened the community treasury.

In this same year, the Harmonists won a significant legal victory in Pennsylvania when one George G. Müller in Pittsburgh had an attachment of about $6,000 served on Abraham Ziegler, the purchaser of Harmonie, Pennsylvania, and lost his suit to recover wages for labor and services while he was a member of the Harmonist Society in that town. The court's decision in the Müller case established a precedent that gave the Harmonist leaders confidence in dealing with any future troublemakers within the society.

9

From the Harmonists' years in Indiana survives another example of the persistence of myth entangled in their history, a bit of local gossip that annoyed them the rest of their days almost as sharply as the story of John Rapp's death; it is the legend associated with two naked human footprints on a limestone slab that is still to be seen in New Harmony in the yard of Father Rapp's home at the corner of Church and Main. Today's visitors to the town always hear the story. Father Rapp, it is said, brought the stone from St. Louis and told his people the footprints were Gabriel's, made when Gabriel came down from heaven to advise him about the conduct of their affairs.

After hearing this story, a sightseer in New Harmony will not find himself much further enlightened about the footprints if he consults historians. George B. Lockwood calls the stone "Gabriel's Rock," repeats the legend of Father Rapp and the angel, quotes a description of the footprints by Schoolcraft but omits Schoolcraft's information about their origin, quotes also the Duke of Saxe-Weimar Eisenach, who said, "This piece of stone was hewed out of a rock near St. Louis and sold to Mr. Rapp," and then concludes that the Duke's "theory" seems to have the weight of authority. Marguerite Young, who seems to have been hoaxed by a New Harmony newspaper editor in the 1940's into believing he was a stone mason hired each year to "restore" the footprints with a cold chisel, leaves the matter of Father Rapp's abuse of them up to her readers' imagination. The WPA Guide to Indiana hedges with the statement that "the truth of the matter seems to be that Frederick Rapp . . . bought the rock near St. Louis." Partisan historians of the German Harmonists, like John S. Duss, are so busy with angry denials of the Gabriel legend that they neglect to document their arguments.

The curious thing about the vagueness and speculation regarding the footprints is that the authentic story of the origin of the limestone slabs and the reason for their purchase has been available from the beginning. In 1822, Henry R. Schoolcraft published an article in the *American Journal of Science and Arts,* entitled "Remarks on the Prints of Human Feet observed in the secondary limestone of the Mississippi Valley," in which he says: "These prints appear to have been noticed by the French soon after they penetrated into that country. . . . But no person appears to have entertained the idea of raising them from the quarry with a view to preservation until Mr. Rappe visited that place five or six years ago. . . . This determination was no sooner known than popular sentiments began to arraign his motives and people were ready to attribute to religous fanaticism or arch deception, what was, more probably, a mere act of momentary caprice, or settled taste. His followers, it was said, were to regard these footprints as the sacred impress of the feet of our Saviour. Few persons thought of interposing a charitable remark in favour of religious tenets, of which we can judge only by the peaceful, industrious, and devotional lives; the neat and cleanly appearance of those who profess them. Still less could be conceded in favour of a personal taste for objects of natural history or curiosity, of which this act is, at least, a proof."

From Schoolcraft's remarks two things are obvious: first, the legend about Father Rapp's abuse of the footprints began even before the stone reached New Harmony, gossip built upon the assumption that Frederick intended to fool his people with them when he got them home; and second, Frederick Rapp was exhibiting the footprints to visitors only a short while after they were brought to Harmonie, for Schoolcraft goes on to say that he visited the place in the summer of 1821 in the suite of Governor Cass, and Frederick Rapp conducted them to see the curiosity in the Rapp garden.

Schoolcraft probably did not know that in the year of the publication of his article John L. Baker and John Reichart were in Germany not only to collect inheritances for the Harmonist Society but also to bring back, at Frederick Rapp's request, Rhine grapes, books, a camera obscura, astronomic charts, and a new kind of musical instrument called a Jubal horn. Such an assortment of articles certainly attests to the "personal taste for objects of natural history and curiosity" that Schoolcraft ascribes to Rapp.

Perhaps not so much because Schoolcraft himself doubted Frederick Rapp's word about the origin of the limestone slab as because he suspected his readers might doubt it, he wrote to Senator Thomas Hart Benton of Missouri for confirmation of the previous existence of the footprint stone on the St. Louis waterfront. In his article, he quotes Benton's reply: "The 'prints' of human feet which you mention I have seen hundreds of times. They were on the uncovered limestone rock in front of the town of St. Louis. . . . The 'prints' were seen when the country was first settled and had the same appearance then as now."

Recently, in the home of Kenneth Dale Owen in New Harmony, a descendant of Robert Owen, a letter was found in an envelope addressed to "R. L. Baker, Esq., Economy, Pa.," and postmarked "Pittsburgh, Oct. 12, 1841," which describes the quarrying of the limestone slab and its shipment to Harmonie on Frederick Rapp's order.

"Dear Sir:

"The letter of Mr. R. Dale Owen of the 20th ultimo inclosed in yours of the 8 inst was duly received by me here. Well Sir, as to the limestone slab that Mr. Fred'r Rapp obtained of me sometime in 1819 at St. Louis: I will tell you it's history— The year after I located in St. Louis during the extreme low water of the Mississipi—I was shown the imprint of human feet that was in the lime-stone rock on the *very margin* of the river and which had been only seen by the old inhabitants *there* but very few times—as it was said by them—that it was not there more than once in a period of ten years *or so,* that the river fell to its *then* stage—This rock was laying at about the centre of the *City Proper,* on the very margin of the river and seemed to have been polished smooth by the attrition of the water. There was no rock laying on it—as it was the lower edge of the stratified lime-stone that reached *by steps* to the bluff of lime stone rock that ranges along the foot of the river lots of the City—This bluff of stratified rock was seemingly from ten to twenty feet high and from 20 to 40 yards from the margin of the river at extreme low water mark *all along the city*—This Bluff has been quarried out and a fine range of three story stone warehouses erected there on the river front. A street too of 10 feet wide has been laid off beside a graduated McAdamized wharf, on the outside of that again, to low water mark.

"A Mr. Jones, who claimed a sort of ownership of this rock as being the first discoverer of it *that Season* was employed by me to cut out the slab for Mr. Frederick Rapp, who was then at St. Louis on a bussiness visit. I paid Jones (to the best of my recollection) 180 dollars for the Slab, and shipped it around to New Harmony to Mr. Rapp. Previous to its being sent away there was an offer of 500 dollars for it, by a 'virtuoso' from some of the Eastern cities; and in consequence of this high estimate of its value, there were many of the citizens strongly disposed to prevent the slab being sent away from the city.

"I know of no rocks along that margin of a soft and plastic nature, that seems to be in a process of consolidation; but the opinion was well grounded *there,* at *that* time, that the imprint of the two human feet had been made on the rock when it was *soft alluvium mud.*

"I never saw or heard of any imprint of human feet along there,—or anywhere else, save on this rock. But I recollect of remarking in many of the steps of the smooth rock along near the same place from which this slab had been taken out the numerous imprints of turkey, deer & Buffalo feet. I often looked to find human imprinted feet but was unsuccessful.

"Mr. Owen asks what was the height above the Mississipi from where the slab was taken out. Now if he had not that question already answered, I say, that the slab was cut out from the very margin of the lowest water stage, and I think it was about 20 feet lower than the exposed bottom of the Bluff that ranges to some 20 to 40 yards off the river margin, it was with some difficulty that we could ride along the shore in consequence of its declivity.

"If hereafter Mr. Owen should require any further information from me I will always be found at Cincinnati & would with pleasure answer him or our mutual acquaintance Doct Locke of that city—

"Respectfully yours,
"Paul Anderson"

Although this letter itself has been mislaid for many years, its contents have been available to historians since July, 1842, when, again in the *American Journal of Science and Arts,* David Dale Owen, a son of Robert Owen, published a large part of it along with his observations on the nature of the footprints. In his article, entitled "Regarding Human Foot-Prints in Solid Limestone," David Dale Owen, like Schoolcraft before him, was more interested in the geological history of the stone and the origin of the footprints than in Frederick Rapp's purchase of them or any legends about Father Rapp and the Angel Gabriel.

Schoolcraft thought the prints were made by human feet, but Owen, a geologist, believed they were artificial. In support of his belief, he offered four arguments:

1. The footprints are not continuous, but isolated, revealing no course that the man could have taken to reach the spot where he stood.

2. This seems to be a solitary instance of footprints in limestone.

3. It is difficult to conceive of a sudden consolidation of compact limestone rock, after having received, while in a plastic state, such impressions.

4. Because of the age, nature, and position of the rock and because no human remains whatever have hitherto been discovered in any similar formations, it seems unlikely that the prints were made by human feet.

Owen's argument is fortified further by the fact that the

St. Louis area was covered by a shallow sea at the time of the formation of limestone. In answer to Schoolcraft's point that iron tools had not yet been invented at the time when the footprints were made, Owen writes, "It appears to me much less improbable that some aboriginal artist should have exhibited unlooked for skill in intagliating a rock, than that a man should have been coeval with crustacea." People capable of making arrowheads out of flint, he reasoned, must certainly have had tools capable of cutting out a small fraction of an inch of limestone.

In a desperate moment Father Rapp might have been tempted by that old serpent to say that the mysterious footprints were Gabriel's or even the Lord's, but it is unlikely that he would have yielded to such a temptation. The legend had already been invented before he saw the stone and had probably preceded the footprints to Harmonie. Father Rapp was not so stupid as to use a story that his people had already heard from their enemies, or would certainly hear soon, even though the Devil might have been stupid enough to think he would do so. What is more, there were few, if any, desperate moments for the leader of the Harmonists in the year 1819. His people were prospering that year, and yet there was still plenty to keep them occupied before they were ready for the millennium. They had little time for restlessness or dissension. Finally, if George Rapp had indeed been so tempted and in a moment of weakness had yielded, his adopted son would have had to go along with the hoax. Certainly Frederick Rapp would not have been showing the stone to strangers two years later, telling them where he got it and how much he paid for it and retailing the gossip to them.

That "virtuoso" mentioned in Paul Anderson's letter, that troublemaking slicker "from some of the Eastern cities," with the alleged five hundred dollars burning a hole in his pocket, was probably at the bottom of the whole affair. But whether or not it was he who invented the gossip about George Rapp and Gabriel, the gossip stuck and annoyed the Harmonists to the end of their days. In our present century, thirty years after the final dissolution of the Harmony Society, John S. Duss was still protesting about what he called "this damnphoolishness," and a lady descendant of Robert Owen, who was much respected in New Harmony and something of a historian herself, was apologizing to the last of the Harmonists' trustees about the persistence of the legend, saying, "I wish at least we could dispose of the rock."

10

Within a few years after the purchase of the rock, Father Rapp could indeed have used the footprints to his advantage if there had been any chance of his followers believing him. Again the Harmonists had got too far ahead of the Lord's schedule for the millennium, just as they had done in old Harmonie on the Connoquenessing. They were ready, but He was not.

By 1822, all the essential buildings of Harmonie on the Wabash were completed, including the fine frame church with its steeple. Flatboats loaded to the gunnels were leaving regularly for New Orleans. Brother Baker and Brother Reichart were back from Germany with the twenty thousand gulden in inheritances and the astronomical charts and the Jubal horn. The one hundred and thirty new members of the community from Germany had settled into the Harmonist routine after signing away their rights to claim any wages or compensation if they chose to leave the society. Troublemaking George G. Müller had lost his suit for such compensation in Pittsburgh. And Frederick Rapp was getting ready to offer money to the state at six per cent. Once more, as in old Harmonie on Connoquenessing Creek, the Harmonists had more time on their hands than was good for them; it was that old serpent, not the millennium, that was just around the corner.

About this time, William Newnham Blane, an English traveler, reported concerning the Harmonists that "the only occasion on which they are all called out is in the event of sudden bad weather, when the hay or corn is cut, but not carried." Perhaps more ominous still was his observation that "during the whole time I was at Harmonie I never saw one of them laugh." There is nothing like a little laughter for putting the Devil out of countenance, and maybe that is what Gabriel would have told Father Rapp if he had visited him at this time.

If ever Father Rapp needed advice from an angel, he needed it by 1822, but by that time the footprint stone had been around for so long that it would not have fooled the simplest peasant in his flock. It had even got itself written up in Professor Benjamin Silliman's *Journal,* as everyone in Harmonie knew. The few who could read English had pored over the article and Mr. Schoolcraft's fine drawing of the footprints bound between the *Journal's* covers. The Harmonists either read or heard everything that was written or said about them. That was one of their troubles; for chiliasts convinced that they were on the right road to Zion they were extremely sensitive to both praise and blame.

In lieu of descending angels Father Rapp was finally visited by a dream, and for a while the situation in Harmonie was eased. Three times he dreamed that the Lord wanted his people to build a new church beside the old one, and each time the specifications were given to him in detail, and although he was neither an engineer nor an architect, he remembered the specifications accurately. In a short while, the idle hands of the Harmonists were busy again.

But the new brick church was too quickly built, complete with its inspiring pillars of cherry, walnut, and sassafras and the rose over its doorway, carved and gilded by Frederick Rapp's own hand. In less than no time, the Harmonists were bargaining for a fine organ in the East, although they never actually made the purchase. Once more, idleness and, with idleness, that ever-lurking serpent threatened the community.

In the fall of 1822, answering an inquiry about Harmonie, Frederick Rapp insisted that "our community stands proud, firm, and immovable upon its rock of truth." But Frederick was nonetheless uneasy. His people were not only idle, they were restless, now that the hardest of their labors were behind them. They were beginning to wonder why they should not enjoy the fruits of those labors, wear the fine cloth they made, drink more freely of their own beverages, instead of selling them all for others to enjoy. Already the Hoosier climate, so mild and enervating, encouraged them to slow down in their assigned tasks. They might soon become chronically lazy, like their neighbors.

What was more, the western land had not developed as Frederick had expected nor in the direction that he had foreseen. Certainly it had not kept pace with the Harmonists' own development. Even though Harmonie was on a river, the best markets were still too far away. Nor was there much that could be done with the money that settled in the community till. Frederick had long ago abandoned his scheme to buy as much silver as possible "at several per cent premium," and, instead, he was now complaining that "worse than robbery is the depreciation of the state paper." Harmonie was prosperous enough as an agricultural operation, but Frederick Rapp was a man who dreamed of manufactures on a large scale and of high finance.

Finally, the neighbors in Indiana were no more friendly

than the neighbors in Pennsylvania had been. True, they had not yet trampled the Harmonists' gardens nor openly accused the spiritual leader of the community of vicious acts, but they had heard all the ugly rumors from Pennsylvania and invented a few of their own and there was constant whispering among them. "Immovable" as the society was "upon its rock of truth," the time had come to move it.

In the winter of 1823–1824, George Rapp and his associates bought a printing press and installed it in their schoolhouse for Johann Christoph Müller, the schoolmaster, to operate. He was to print Father Rapp's *Gedanken* and Frederick Rapp's English translation and emendation of that treatise, and maybe, with the help of Isaac Blackford, a lawyer at Vincennes, that work could be polished into a readable prose that would enlighten the outside world about Harmonist beliefs and purposes and so reduce the animosity.

Meantime, although the decision to move had been made, business must go on as usual. Jonathan Lenz and others continued to set out for New Orleans in their richly burdened flatboats, and although the English mills could underprice the factory on Steam Mill Street, that factory continued to weave good woolen cloth. The value of land too must not be overlooked. As late as August 1, 1824, George Rapp and his associates bought some 1,500 additional acres, presumably for speculation, since by that time Frederick Rapp had already commissioned Richard Flower of Albion, Illinois, to advertise the town for sale in England and had himself gone back to Pennsylvania and bought a tract of 3,000 acres on the Ohio River eighteen miles north of Pittsburgh for the start of a new community. Indeed by August, 1824, the first contingent of the Harmonists had already left for Pennsylvania on the steamboat *Ploughboy,* taking with them $6,633.40 worth of meticulously inventoried woolens, cottons, family goods, shoes, soap, tallow, whiskey, brandy, flaxseed oil, molasses, leather, shovels, turpentine, glass, nails, rope, plough lines, and German scythes. To the last it was necessary to keep the idle hands busy.

Father Rapp went with that first contingent and wrote back to the remaining members on the banks of the Wabash the first day after he arrived in their new home, which was to be called Economy: "I consider this place the most healthful in America. . . . What we are doing, we do for you, and what you do, you do for us." That Father Rapp kept the departed Harmonists busy in Economy goes without saying.

At Economy, Pennsylvania, that fall the Harmonists built a steamboat and named it the *William Penn*. Abishai Way, their Pittsburgh agent, engaged a captain for them, one Francis Erwin, at sixty dollars per month "while running." Of Erwin, Way wrote to Frederick Rapp, "He is to perform the duties of Master and first pilot, but as he has not been much in what is called genteel company he wishes to be excused from the cabin duties, usually performed by the Capt."

The *William Penn* and the *Ploughboy* and two other steamboats, the *Bolivar* and the *Phoenix*, transported most of the remainder of the society from Harmonie, Indiana, to Economy, Pennsylvania, although a few traveled east by Conestoga wagon. The last group of Württembergers left the town on the Wabash in the summer of 1825. Six months before, at Christmas time, Robert Owen of New Lanark, Scotland, had agreed to buy the Indiana town and some of its appurtenances and had renamed it New Harmony.

The only written record of themselves that the Württembergers left behind for the inveterate recorders of the inner life who took over their town was scrawled with chalk in German under the stairway in No. 2.

"In the 24th of May, 1824, we have departed. Lord, with Thy great help and goodness, in body and soul, protect us."

These words are still legible on the rough wood where they were written.

11

What was the true character of these Württembergers who came to await the millennium in the New World and in the course of their waiting created three thriving little new worlds of their own? Was the harmony that they wrought in Pennsylvania, removed to Indiana, and brought back to Pennsylvania all that it appeared to them to be, as like unto the kingdom of heaven as anything that could be fashioned on this earth by mortal men? Or was it a hell for those who lived in it, as the people of Pennsylvania warned little Christina Vogt it would be before she left to join her family in Indiana? How were these Harmonists able to renounce all worldly possessions and in so doing accumulate a fortune beyond the talents or the imaginations of most men of their day? Were they what they professed to be, dedicated to the common welfare with no self-interest beyond the salvation of their souls, innocent children of God inspired by the chiliastic dream? Or were they only more intelligent than those around them, shrewder, given to sharper practices, more industrious? Or were they, as some have contended, a herd of stupid peasants tricked and driven by a few unscrupulous men whose motives derived from that old serpent and not from divine revelation? What were these Württembergers really like?

When these questions are asked, there seems at first to be no fixed starting point for an objective answer. The Harmonists left behind them no single universally accepted picture of themselves. They had no talent for creating a public image, that effect so dubiously sought after today by organizations as well as individuals. They never proselytized. Indeed they were always ill at ease with outsiders. The result is that contemporary accounts of them are at variance.

Their infelicity among strangers is more understandable when it is remembered that their two chief preoccupations were money-making and the exclusive salvation of their own souls. Neither of these two pursuits lends itself to openheartedness in relation to others. Their private correspondence is mostly commercial and parochial and reveals little more about them than a talent for bargaining and prospering in spite of awkwardness in their adopted country's language and a lack of elegance in their own. By contrast with the volubility of the society that succeeded them in New Harmony, whose members seldom had a thought without setting it down on paper and preserving the paper for posterity, there seems to be an almost deliberate absence of self-portrayal in the written records of the Harmonists. To see them one must look between the lines.

This absence of an original image to work from may be one of the reasons why the tellers of the New Harmony story have never settled upon a commonly accepted appraisal of the founders of the town. With inordinate partisan praise on the one hand and with equally partisan neglect or indifference on the other, they have seldom aimed squarely at the truth. Indeed historians have not even agreed upon a name for these chiliasts. Some consistently call them "Rappites," which is the name their successors in New Harmony tagged them with; others call them "Harmonists," which is the name of their own choosing.

One example of the short shrift a writer can give the Harmonists is George B. Lockwood's *The New Harmony Movement*. Published in 1905, it has long been the standard full-length treatment of the New Harmony story; and yet it devotes to "the Rappites" only thirty-five of its three hundred and seventy-seven pages. Lockwood seems to respect the Harmonists for what they built on the banks of the Wabash, but he shows very little interest in what they were. In fact, he gives the total impression that they were not much, a flock of sheep herded by a shadowy shepherd who was "cheerful and kindly" but not above "playing on the superstitions of the peasantry" in order to achieve his not always pious or altruistic ends.

On the other hand, there are books about the Harmonists that only glorify them. In *The Harmony Society,* published in 1954, Christiana F. Knoedler, who spent her childhood in the final community in Pennsylvania, is rhapsodic about the Germans' way of life. Aaron Williams's *The Harmony Society at Economy, Pennsylvania,* written in 1866 as a defense against "a slanderous article in the *Atlantic Monthly,*" gives the impression that the millennium came when the first articles of association were signed. In *George Rapp and His Associates*— a four-hour lecture that stunned the people of New Harmony at their Centennial celebration in 1914—John S. Duss, one of the last two members of the society, takes still another partisan tack. Laying aside Christian charity, he is angrily at odds with all the non-Harmonist world in an emotional defense of Harmonist virtues.

Some historians have approached the subject of New Harmony only to abandon their labors in defeat or dismay over the tangled problem of what these communists were like. Others have compromised by writing books about Utopias in general, or books about the region, into which they have tucked a few pages or a chapter or two about New Harmony. One author—Marguerite Young, whose *Angel in the Forest* appeared in 1945—converted the chiliastic dream, both "Rappite" and "Owenite," into something that has been variously called a novel and a prose-poem, but hardly deserves to be called a history since Miss Young is so free with facts that she makes the Wabash River flow backwards.

The seeker after the truth about the Harmonists will do best to take a leaf out of George Rapp's own book. When the service proves an empty show, he must go to the fountainhead of intuition within himself for understanding—or, as a chiliast of another sort once said, plant himself firmly on his instincts and there abide. Then maybe the truth will come round to him. Certainly the ultimate truth about human beings has never been found in a cross index of references, explanatory footnotes, polemics, or even in a "definitive" analysis.

One key to the Harmonists' character lies in the words George Rapp wrote to Frederick Reichert before the emigrations from Germany began.

You must not urge anyone to come.

Rapp wrote these words to Frederick privately. He was not thinking of a public image, the impression that he would make upon outsiders. He meant exactly what he said. "You must not urge anyone to come—it is a long and perilous journey." And since Frederick Reichert was a shrewd and practical man and proved himself the rest of his life loyal to George Rapp there can be little doubt that he obeyed Rapp's injunction. Therefore, it can be concluded that the Württembergers were not dragooned into coming to America, as some have asserted. They volunteered. Some of them may indeed have slipped past Frederick's careful scrutiny and come for the wrong reasons— to escape Napoleon's conscription, to evade responsibilities at home, in the spirit of adventure, or in the hope of getting something for nothing; but none of them came because he was coerced or deceived.

But if this was so, it will then be asked, why have so many observers and historians regarded the Harmonists as little better than a corps of slave labor, a herd of stupid sheep led by self-interested shepherds? If it could be easily proved otherwise, why did this slander haunt the society throughout the whole century of its existence?

The answer is that it was not altogether a slander. After all, Frederick Reichert was selecting a working society to transplant to the New World. He was not trying to create the millennium in advance of the Lord's plan. That was to come in the Lord's own good time, to be waited for and worked for, as George Rapp said. Reichert no doubt searched candidates' souls for imperfections, but their intellects were another matter. To have chosen only the highly intelligent would have been impractical. Someone had to do the hard labor of the society, do it well, and without complaining. There were dullards aboard the *Atlantic* and the *Aurora* and the *Margaret,* because dullards were needed to perform dull work that intellectual men would have rebelled against.

Outsiders found it difficult to distinguish the stupid from the clever in the ranks of the Harmonist Society because of the uniform dress the Württembergers wore. There is nothing like a uniform to reduce a crowd to its lowest common denominator. But even so, the dullards could not have been mere dunces, for a dunce would have been a menace to the general welfare; and certainly even such dullards as Reichert selected were in a small minority, for the work that lay ahead in America and the achievements the Harmonists finally attained required clever heads as well as clever hands. Of the five hundred who signed Harmonie, Indiana, over to Robert Owen, only thirty-nine were unable to write their names. For that time and place, this was a very low rate of illiteracy.

Curiously enough, it was the Harmonists themselves—some of them, that is—who originated the slander about the ovine stupidity of the Württembergers. When the first articles of association were drawn up in Pennsylvania, about ten of the wealthier families who had come to join the society refused to sign. After they departed from Harmonie, they naturally felt they had to justify their *volte-face* to themselves and to the outside world, and the obvious justification was that Rapp's terms were too harsh and tyrannical for intelligent men to agree to.

The inevitable inference to be drawn from this explanation was that those who did sign were stupid, were indeed fools.

It was not long until the slander was abetted by those who did sign. Misery and dissension soon arose in their midst. In August, 1805, George Rapp wrote to his adopted son, who was away on business, that the community had gone a long time without bread and the principal food was the "cookables" from the gardens. By 1806, the leaders of the community were desperately wishing they could move farther west and start all over. It was at this time that they wrote their pathetic appeal to Thomas Jefferson. By this time the Rapps had also entered into a dispute with the neighboring town of Zelienople, which was owned by the man who had sold them their land. The quarrel was over the establishment of a post office on the road from Pittsburgh to Lake Erie, and although it was eventually settled in Harmonie's favor, the indiscreet talk of members of the community, who were anxious about the wrangle and the hardships of their society, gave rise to a rumor that the society was on the verge of collapse. This rumor stirred the Harmonists' neighbors to distrust the whole Harmonist movement and the motives of its leaders.

Distrust so planted in the minds of outsiders was not allayed when the Harmonists at last began to prosper. Instead, it was aggravated by the envy this prosperity inspired. Such envy was especially prevalent after the Harmonists moved to Indiana and created a small paradise in the wilderness unlike anything that existed roundabout. Backwoodsmen living in squalor in the Ohio and Wabash valleys, subsisting mainly on game and corndodgers, could only be jealous of neighbors who inhabited such a spacious flowering village as Harmonie, where people lived in brick houses that were warm in winter and cool in summer, fared well at table, and prospered in all their endeavors.

THE ANGEL AND THE SERPENT

One English traveler who passed through Harmonie, Indiana, in 1819, saw no comfortable dwellings in the forest surrounding the town but only "miserable little log-holes, having neither springs nor mill-streams." But "on the Harmony lands and fields, of great size," he saw "wheat, finer and thicker, planted with two bushels, than in England with three and a half bushels per acre." In the town itself he found "a large and comfortable brick tavern, the best and cleanest which I had seen in Indiana," and he slept "in a good clean bed." Another Englishman, visiting the town the previous year, had reported that "the tavern is conducted in the most orderly and cleanly manner that a tavern can be in America, where men spit *every where,* and almost on *every thing.*" He discovered that "the country people hate the Harmonists very much, because they permit no drunkenness in their taverns." Morris Birkbeck, on a trip through southern Indiana in 1817, observed that the woodsmen, who lived in small dark cabins, were "tall and pale, like vegetables that grow in a vault, pining for light," whereas in Harmonie the people "exhibited so much health, and peace, and neatness in their persons, that we could not but exclaim." Small wonder that the cabin-dwellers in the meager clearings of southern Indiana preferred to think the worst of their German neighbors.

The attitude of the Harmonists toward their neighbors did nothing to soften the resentment that their better way of life earned for them. The Germans kept to themselves. They were uncooperative, refusing to let their town become the county seat. They sought special privileges, asking for lower fines for themselves when they would not serve in the militia. They were inhospitable, except to persons of importance or those who could be of use to them. Perhaps worst of all in the eyes of their neighbors, they showed no interest in learning English (George Rapp himself never mastered the language), and when questions were asked about their religion and their communal organization, they were taciturn and sometimes rude.

William Faux heard a stranger in the Harmonie tavern ask the landlord what religion the community professed. "In broken English, and rather crossly, he replied, 'Dat's no matter; they are all satisfied people.' " The man then asked whether strangers would be permitted to go to the village church service the next day, and the answer was a curt *no*. "This," Faux remarked in his diary, "is unprecedented in the civilized world."

Henry Schoolcraft, after a visit to Harmonie in July, 1821, reported, "We have vainly sought to draw from them the mysterious ties by which a community of 900 souls, possessing all property in common, are influenced to dwell together in apparent unity and fraternal love. . . . The religious tenets which they profess, the studious silence maintained, and their evasive replies when questioned on the subject, permitted us only to learn that they are, in the main, Lutherans." When Schoolcraft asked his Harmonist guide whether there were any religious differences among them before they emigrated, the guide said only, " 'Wir sind eins.' " (We are one.)

Two years later, William Hebert encountered the same kind of rebuff. When he asked the keeper of the "house of private entertainment" if the Harmonists were "not desirous of increasing the number of their society," the answer was, " 'Not by strangers.' "A friend of Hebert's pursued the inquiry further. Would they, he asked, welcome an increase of numbers from among their own countrymen? The innkeeper replied that they considered Germans who were not of their faith equally strangers to them with Americans and Englishmen. " 'That is the answer,' the innkeeper said, implying that the answer he had given us was *'the answer'* to all inquiries."

Like the neighboring backwoodsmen, such travelers left the village with mixed feelings about the society. Later, in their published remarks, they contributed to the general impression of the German communists that popular gossip had already created. Morris Birkbeck, who was the most sympathetically predisposed toward them and who for a while engaged in satisfactory business dealings with them, admired the orderliness and prosperity of Harmonie; but after Frederick Rapp charged him that extra four hundred dollars on the protested drafts, he was not quite convinced that the leaders of the society were sincere. Elias Pym Fordham concluded that "they must be in the chains of superstition, though Rapp professes to govern them only by the Bible, and they certainly seem the perfection of obedience and morality. People who have left them say, that Rapp preaches, that if they quit the society, they will be damned, for his way is the only way to Heaven. He does much by signs, and by an impressive manner, stretching out his arm, which he says is the arm of God." Hebert called them "an ignorant and priest-ridden set of people" and ended by preferring the "Shaking Quakers," if only because "they are not merchants or money-changers, and when visited by strangers, entertain them gratis. This you will allow to be really respectable."

Even the Harmonists' compatriot, Bernhard, Duke of Saxe-Weimar Eisenach, could not resist an invidious comparison when he visited New Harmony the year after Robert Owen bought the town. "Mr. Owen then conducted me to Rapp's former dwelling," the Duke recalled in his *Travels Through North America, during the year 1825 and 1826,* "a large, well-built brick house, with two lightning rods. The man of God, it appears, took especial care of himself; his house was by far the best in the place, surrounded by a garden with a flight of stone steps, and the only one furnished with lightning rods. Mr. Owen, on the contrary, contented himself with a small apartment in the same tavern where I lodged."

(What the Duke neglected to note, of course, was that George Rapp was a permanent resident in his community, whereas Robert Owen was never anything more than a transient in the community he had bought. Even so, within a few years after the Duke's visit, Owen's family built a house at the edge of town with a façade one hundred and twenty-five feet long, a house so large that, when it was finally torn down, five two-story houses and two smaller ones were constructed out of the materials that came from it.)

There is frequent evidence that the "Owenites" encouraged the popular belief that their German predecessors were stupid peasants abused by a few tyrannical hypocrites in authority. It is human nature to wish to appear superior to one's predecessor, especially if he has been in any sense a competitor, and the members of the second group of communists in New Harmony were pre-eminently human in spite of their high ideals. Moreover, their theory of communism was entirely different from that practiced by the Württembergers, and so, whether they acknowledged it or not, there was a strong professional rivalry between them.

Certainly these Württembergers were imbued with the German's respect for authority—his obsequious submission to it when it is exercised by others and his ruthless passion for it when it is vested in himself; and they were also fully charged with the German's congenital mysticism, which is self-hypnotic and can be easily translated into mass hysteria. There is some truth in Joseph Conrad's remark that the German genius is "a hypnotizing power over half-baked souls and half-lighted minds." But this is not the whole truth. Among the Harmonists, as in all societies, there were those in whose minds glowed very little illumination, but they were not all sheep. Nor were their leaders hypocrites. Although, being human, they occasionally took advantage of their superior natural endowments for what they had convinced themselves was the people's good, the records show that, whatever else they did or did not do, the leaders of the Harmonists never took any private profit from the common good at this period in their history.

For some reason, men find it easier to give the devil his due than to grant the self-righteous their special virtues. It is unfortunate that men of good will are suspicious when they encounter faith in an unfamiliar form in others and immediately accuse its adherents of consorting with the devil. That old serpent certainly played a role among the men and women who founded Harmonie in 1814. He seemed most often to appear when there was the smell of money in the air. But the Harmonists never ceased looking in the direction of the angels when they lived on the shores of the Wabash. Perhaps that is why they did not always notice the serpent at their feet.

Part Two

⋘§⋙

The Community of
Equality

12

GEORGE RAPP founded New Harmony, Indiana, with the intention of awaiting the millennium there; Robert Owen came to the town believing he brought the millennium with him. Where Rapp was willing to leave the second creation up to the Lord, Owen took the responsibility for it wholly upon himself. It seems paradoxical that what the visitor sees in New Harmony today—its careful planning, its sturdy buildings and homes—is the work of the man who came expecting the imminent end of the world, while the man who came to create a new world left nothing visible or tangible. But the spirit of New Harmony that the visitor becomes aware of, if he lingers long enough, is the legacy of Robert Owen.

The story of Robert Owen's early life reads like a success story by Horatio Alger. As told by Robert Owen *Himself,* as he advertises his autobiography on its title page, the story loses nothing that Horatio Alger might have put into it, for modesty never stood between Owen and the contemplation of his own virtues. At the very outset, in a preface, the hero credits himself with "the greatest discovery that man has made for the universal happiness of the human race," and observes that "the mission of my life appears to be to prepare the population of the world to understand the vast importance of the second creation of humanity."

Owen was born in Newtown, Montgomeryshire, North Wales, in 1771, the son of a saddler and youngest-but-one of a family of seven children. By his own admission, he was the brightest of the lot, always the first at school and the first at home. By the time he was seven years old, his schoolmaster, a Mr. Thickness, despaired of teaching the boy anything more and asked him to become his assistant. After that, Owen remarks, his remaining years in school were a waste, except that he learned the habit of teaching others, which he practiced the rest of his life.

Owen says that during his school years he read a book a day and believed every word he read. Apparently he read no history, for ignorance of history was always evident in his proposals for reforming the world. As one of his sons later put it, he showed a "lack of familiarity with precedent authorities." However, there must have been a large dose of theology in Robert Owen's early reading, because he says he ceased believing in the superiority of the Christian religion at the age of nine, although, paradoxically, he was at that time called "the little preacher." He even wrote three sermons at that age, but later, finding that Laurence Sterne had written three that were almost like them, he burned his own for fear he might be considered a plagiarist.

Again by his own admission, young Robert was the most admired boy in Newtown and the best dancer in his dancing class, and from his eighth year until he left home his parents never made an important decision without first consulting him. When he finally left for London at the age of ten, he called upon and took leave of everyone in Newtown, because he "knew and was known by every man, woman, and child in town." He does not record whether or not his fellow townsmen were sorry to see him go.

Egotistical as Owen's estimate of his own talents is, it is substantiated by his precocious success in business. He left Wales with only his coach fare to London and forty shillings in his pocket, and by the time he was twenty-six, with no assistance beyond a single loan of one hundred pounds from a brother, he was a one-third owner of the largest and most prosperous textile mill in Scotland. Soon thereafter he was the most famous industrialist in the British Isles and one of the wealthiest.

Owen began his career at the age of ten by working for a Scot named McGuffog who kept a fabric shop in Lancashire. Within a year or so, he moved to a similar shop in London. Here his working day commenced at eight in the morning and he stayed on the job frequently until two the next morning. In the summer, he got up at three or four in the morning and walked in the park until the shop opened—"to think, read, and study." A byproduct of these early-morning meditations was a letter that he wrote at the age of thirteen to the Prime Minister urging government measures to enforce a better keeping of the Sabbath; he had observed that Sunday drunkenness was reducing the efficiency of the working class on Mondays. Ten days after he posted the letter, a government proclamation recommended that the Sabbath be more strictly enforced. Owen was never able to prove, however, that the proclamation was a result of his suggestion.

At eighteen, with three spinning mules in his possession, Robert Owen was in business for himself, making yarn for muslin. At twenty, he became the manager of five hundred mill hands in Manchester at a salary of three hundred pounds a year. "My name," he says at this point in his life, "was now up for being the first fine cotton spinner in the world." Apparently he was not exaggerating.

In Manchester, Owen's social and intellectual life broadened. He joined the Manchester Literary and Philosophical Society and, with members of the faculty of Manchester College, formed a small discussion group that included young Samuel Taylor Coleridge. On one occasion, meeting Coleridge head-on in a debate about religion, Owen at least outtalked the voluble poet if he did not convince him, proving, if nothing else, that he was already one of the most uninterruptible monologists of his day. About this same time, Owen mounted a horse for the first time in his life and led all the experienced hunters in the field and was in at every kill. Perhaps of more enduring credit to the enterprising young man at this period was the loan of money he made to Robert Fulton in recognition of the inventor's promise at the beginning of his career.

But it was love as much as financial wizardry and social and intellectual initiative that brought Owen to the ownership of the great textile mill in New Lanark, Scotland, with which his name is associated in the history of industrial reform. On a tour of inspection for his Manchester firm, he met in Glasgow the daughter of David Dale, owner of the New Lanark plant. Characteristically, Owen reversed the classic procedure in such circumstances; he did not marry the boss's daughter and inherit the business, he bought the business and then persuaded the old man to let him marry the girl.

Owen and Ann Caroline Dale were wed in 1799, and Owen took over management at New Lanark on January 1, 1800. David Dale, a devout Presbyterian, said to his new son-in-law, by this time a professed atheist, "Thou needest be very kind, for thou art very positive."

Very kind Robert Owen seems aways to have been, remaining throughout his life positive and egotistical also. Although one of his motives for wanting to reform the world was to improve industrial efficiency and increase profits, he was guided also by a profound concern for the welfare of human beings and, at the outset at least, exhibited great patience and generosity in his efforts to ameliorate their lot. At New Lanark, he was distressed by the intemperance of the workers and the squalor and ignorance in which they lived. A quarter of a century later, in America, he was no longer able to see what was directly under his nose and lived in a vague euphoria of good intentions; but, even so, on the rare occasions when he visited the site of his social experiment at New Harmony, the warmth of his presence never failed to revive the spirits of his confused and squabbling disciples.

In 1800, New Lanark was inhabited by about fourteen hundred families and some five hundred pauper children who had been imported under contract to work in the mill according to the custom of the times. Owen deplored the practice of employing children in textile mills at the age of six, and sometimes even five, and working them fourteen hours a day. By changing partners and ultimately acquiring full control at New Lanark, he eventually raised the minimum age to ten in the face of competition with other millowners who continued to employ younger children, but he was never able to reduce the working day to less than ten and three-quarters hours.

Immediately after Owen took over at New Lanark, he set about constructing roomier houses for his workers, removing the dunghills from their front dooryards and conducting regular inspections of housekeeping with special rewards for improvement. He purchased better goods to be sold in the company stores and saw to it that there was an adequate supply of fuel, food, and clothing for everyone. Where the Germans in Harmonie, Indiana, had eased the workers' lot with flowers in vases, Owen set up at each workbench in his New Lanark mill a device for recording his employees' deportment. This "silent monitor" was a four-sided piece of wood, each side colored and numbered. Black and No. 4 denoted *bad* conduct; blue and No. 3, *indifferent;* yellow and No. 2, *good;* white and No. 1, *excellent.* Soon the results of Owen's efforts, in spite of sullen opposition among the workers in the beginning, were a general improvement in public health, decrease of vice, and increase of production.

Perhaps Owen would never have overcome the workers' opposition as he finally did if Thomas Jefferson had not inadvertently helped him by closing American ports to export trade about the time the Welshman took over the New Lanark mill. Owen converted into a blessing this embargo that seemed to others like a blow. With the supply of American cotton to England cut off, he had to close his mill like all the other British textile manufacturers, but unlike them he paid his workers full wages all the while they were laid off. When at last the embargo was lifted, he had the confidence and loyalty of all his employees.

At the end of eight years of preliminary reform at New Lanark, Owen undertook to rebuild the foundation of the town's social structure by establishing a school in the community in which he could educate children upon the three basic principles that he had conceived as the starting point for reforming the human race:

"1. Man does not form his own character; it is formed for him by the circuumstances that surround him.

"2. Man is not a fit subject for praise or blame.

"3. Any general character, good or bad, may be given to the world, by applying means which are, to a great extent, under the control of human government."

Owen believed that if the world was to be made over it was first of all necessary to take children away from their parents and thus break the chain of training in the accumulated wrong habits and superstitions of the ages. Children entered the New Lanark school at the age of two, and thus the school became the first infant school in history. The children "were not to be annoyed with books," for Owen believed books were only a hindrance to the formation of character before the age of ten. No attempt was made to teach the pupils reading or writing, not even their letters. Objects were their textbooks—natural objects mostly, from gardens, fields and woods, and maps and paintings of objects of nature; but even these objects were not explained until the pupils' curiosity about them arose naturally and they began to ask questions. So there were no set lessons, and much of the children's time was spent on the playground. Nor was punishment administered for misconduct; the unco-operative child was expected to learn about good and evil from observing the social consequences of his acts.

Later, Owen was to send his own sons to Philipp Emanuel von Fellenberg's "Self-Governing College," which he had ad-mired in Switzerland, and where they were to have among their schoolmates Prince Alexander of Württemberg, a nephew of the Duke who had ruled that country when George Rapp and his followers departed. Emanuel von Fellenberg conducted his school in a castle at Hofwyl, two leagues from Berne, on prin-ciples he had learned from his friend Pestalozzi. The institu-tion included a primary school, an industrial school, and work-shops for improved agricultural instruments. The tuition was $1500 a year, no paltry sum to pay for an education in those days. Among the students were numerous sons of dukes and princes, but coats of arms gave no special privileges. The boys were responsible for their own discipline and democracy was the order of the day.

The New Lanark experiment in education would have had a better chance of success if Robert Owen had concentrated on perfecting his methods and had not advertised success before it was achieved. He invited the world to come and see what he was doing when it was still yet to be done. Robert Dale Owen, one of the sons educated at Hofwyl, reported that between 1815 and 1825, the number of visitors at New Lanark was nearly twenty thousand. The schoolroom became a theatre, the pupils performers, and Robert Owen the publicity agent for the show. It was at this time that he began to develop that inability to stay in one place and to concentrate on one task at a time that was the undoing of all his later projects. Mistaking the word for the deed, he forever after traveled about making speeches, as if the sound of his own voice proclaiming the millennium were the millennium itself.

One of the "superstitions" that Owen wanted to eradicate by education was religion; he believed that religion had caused more suffering than any other factor in the molding of human lives. In his autobiography, he wrote: "There is no sacrifice at any period, which I would not make, that would not have been joyously and willingly made to terminate the existence of religion on earth." Unwittingly, Owen made the most crucial sacrifice of his life in this regard on August 21, 1817, when, at a meeting in London, he turned the attention of the British public away from the constructive application of his reforms by denouncing all the religions of the ages. On that occasion, at the peak of his career, he not only lost his great popular support, he seemed also to lose all sense of proportion. Thenceforth, his *idée fixe* about religion stood between him and reality in everything he undertook, and the course of the rest of his life was downhill, even though the most famous of his experiments—the Community of Equality at New Harmony—still lay ahead of him.

The year 1817 marked the peak of the Harmonists' success in Harmonie on the Wabash, too, for that was the year the hundred and thirty recruits came from Germany. To men like George and Frederick Rapp it was obvious that the only direction men can take from any pinnacle is down and the only way to avert disaster in the descent is for them to fix their vision upon another height to be scaled. Foreseeing what must eventually happen to their Indiana town, the Rapps decided to begin another community back in Pennsylvania long before awkward circumstances forced that choice upon them. Robert Owen, however, did not recognize what had happened to him in England when he made that speech in London; and when he decided seven years later to hazard new fortunes in a foreign

land, he did so because he had no other choice if he was to sal-
vage anything from his own peculiar dream.

Thus the year 1817 was a turning point in the careers of
both the Rapps in Indiana and Robert Owen in England, a
turning point that brought these men together seven years
later in proper frames of mind for the sale of the town on the
Wabash. The Germans were eager to unload a property they
had already all but abandoned; the Welshman was seeking,
more desperately than he knew, another chance to prove that
his theories about man and God were right.

As love had played a role in the purchase of New Lanark at
the turn of the century, so it played a role again in the removal
of Owen's reforming efforts to the New World in 1824. But on
the second occasion, it was not Robert Owen's heart that was
involved; it was his son's. Robert Dale Owen in his early twen-
ties had become enamored of the ten-year-old daughter of a
laborer in New Lanark. Conspiring with his sister Ann, who
recognized his love, he persuaded her to ask their parents to
adopt the girl. This Ann did, and the child became a member
of the Owen household in their countryseat, Braxfield, halfway
up the steep hill north of the mill town. When Richard Flower
appeared at the Owen estate as agent for the sale of the Rapps'
village on the Wabash, the girl was still only thirteen years old
and Robert Dale Owen's future relationship to her was not yet
settled. So, one morning, when his father asked him, "Well,
Robert, what say you—New Lanark or Harmony?" Robert Dale
Owen answered, without hesitation, "Harmony," because, as
he reports in his autobiography, he hoped that "if our family
settled in Western America, it would facilitate my marriage to
Jessie."

Although this strange romance has no further bearing on the
New Harmony story, its denouement deserves a postscript here.
When Jessie was fifteen, young Owen confessed his love to his

mother, and his mother persuaded him to let three more years pass before he made his love known to the girl. During the postponement, while young Owen was in America, his sister Ann died without ever telling Jessie of her brother's love, and Jessie married. Robert Dale Owen did not see Jessie again for thirty years. When finally they met again, both of them married and middle-aged, Jessie told Owen that she had loved him when she was a child and would have waited for him if she had known how he felt about her.

13

The Rapps' agent, Richard Flower, lacked at least one of the qualifications that modern salesmen are expected to have; he was not completely sold on his own merchandise. When he proposed the purchase of Harmonie to Robert Owen, he was astounded by Owen's immediate interest. Unable to conceal his amazement, he said to young Robert Dale Owen, "Does your father *really* think of giving up a position like this, with every comfort and luxury, and taking his family to the wild life of the far west?" The younger Owen remarks in his autobiography at this point that Flower did not realize that Robert Owen's "one ruling desire was for a vast theatre on which to try his plans of social reform."

Robert Dale Owen did not accompany his father and Richard Flower on the trip to America that ensued in the fall of 1824. A whole year was to pass before he made that journey, and he was not to see New Harmony, as it was called by the time he got there, until early in 1826. Someone had to keep store in New Lanark while the advance agent for the social millennium was on the road, and that duty fell to the oldest son. Since it kept him near the little girl he loved, it should not have been an onerous duty. Remaining at home, Robert Dale Owen taught in his father's school and, in the fall of 1824, published a book derived from the experience, *An Outline of the System of Education at New Lanark.*

It was William Owen who made the first transatlantic journey with his father. With the two Owens and Richard Flower there was also an engaging gentleman of thirty-three named Donald Macdonald, who was known as Lord of the Isles of Skye, but who was actually only plain Captain Macdonald of the Royal Engineers on half-pay. Macdonald's diaries give a detailed account of the journey. From them we learn that on the voyage to America on the ship *New York,* Robert Owen expounded his ideas to everyone aboard, morning, noon, and night, all the way across the Atlantic. After the arrival in America, Macdonald's diaries are supplemented by those of William Owen, who began his "journalizing," as he called it, on November 10, 1824. William conscientiously jotted down the morning and evening temperatures and observed, among many other things, that his father spent a great deal of time with the ladies.

In Philadelphia, the Owen party met Madame Marie Duclos Fretageot, a Frenchwoman in charge of an experimental boarding school for girls at the northwest corner of Twelfth and Walnut Streets. This school had been established in 1806 by William Maclure, a Scottish geologist and philanthropist, and was first supervised by Joseph Neef, a former colleague of Pestalozzi. Maclure had already visited New Lanark, where he was impressed by the school's "orderly, cheerful & sober society without any coertion or physical constraint." At the time of Robert Owen's visit in Philadelphia, Maclure was in Paris, having recently left Spain, where he had been forced by the invasion of French troops to abandon an agricultural school that he was setting up near Alicante. Joseph Neef, meantime, had retired from pedagogy and become a farmer in Kentucky. Robert Owen so charmed Madame Fretageot with his plans for a socialist community on the Wabash that she wrote at once enthusiastically to Maclure to interest him in the project.

From Philadelphia, Owen and his son and Captain Macdonald went by steamboat to Baltimore and thence by stage to Washington, where Owen met President James Monroe, President-elect John Quincy Adams, and several members of the Cabinet. Among the latter, John C. Calhoun, the Secretary of War, seemed to impress him most, as "a man of considerable genius." In Washington, Owen also made the acquaintance of some Choctaw and Chickasaw chiefs who had come to the capital dressed in white men's clothing to transact business with the President. To all these men, red and white, Owen explained his plans for redeeming their country from superstition and social inequality, and from each he received courteous attention, if not full comprehension.

In Philadelphia, Owen had got a notice from George Rapp that there were two other prospective buyers of the town of Harmonie and if he did not bring the transaction to a satisfactory close by the end of December the property would be sold to one of them. So the stay in Washington and the conversion of Indians to atheism and Adamses to communism had to be cut short, and on November 28 the Owen party left the capital at three o'clock in the morning and traveled for six days by hackney coach, spring wagon, and stage to Pittsburgh. There, on Saturday, December 4, George Rapp and Robert Owen were introduced to each other by a Pittsburgh glass manufacturer named Benjamin Bakewell, who was interested in establishing a community of equality of his own on the Welshman's specifications.

On that clear and frosty December Saturday, the stolid, burly, white-bearded German mystic and the garrulous, jetty-nosed and bespectacled little Welsh atheist, aged fifty-three, beaver-hatted and wearing a cape, rode in George Rapp's carriage down the valley of the Ohio to the Harmonists' new town of Economy. Captain Macdonald made the trip on horseback in the company of an American Indian named Hunter, whom Owen had picked up in New York and who planned to join the society in Indiana. William Owen, Richard Flower, and several others traveled in a gig. At Economy, they had supper in George Rapp's house, and the next day, Sunday, Robert Owen compromised with his principles long enough to attend the Harmonists' church services across the street.

Macdonald's description of George Rapp and his followers is among the few first-hand impressions of them preserved from this period of their history. "Mr. Rapp," he wrote in his diary, "is a stout healthy active man of sixty-seven. He has a steady determined manner, but very little of that amiable mildness, which a patriarchal life and benevolent principles might be expected to produce. The people appear steady, sober, good-humored and plain in their manners. Their character and expression of countenance is German. They do not appear very lively or intelligent; but of this a stranger cannot after one day's acquaintance, be expected to form a just estimate."

Since George Rapp was engaged in selling his Indiana holdings, he may have appeared somewhat less benevolent to the Lord of the Isles at that time than he might have at another. To young William Owen, wide-eyed with wonder in the New World, the leader of the Harmonists seemed agreeable enough. In fact, William was so naive that he believed his father converted the German patriarch to his atheist's view of the New Moral World that first evening. After the elder Owen finished expounding his ideas, according to William's report, George Rapp declared that he had often said to himself, "My God! is there no man on God's earth who has the same opinions as myself and can help me in my plans? I am lucky now to have come in contact with such an one."

But the "plans" Father Rapp had in mind were probably

his plans to get rid of the Indiana property; certainly they were not his plans for the millennium that he believed imminent, a chiliastic dream quite different from Robert Owen's. Father Rapp was a shrewd businessman. He had more sense than to get into an argument with the very positive little Welshman at this point in their negotiations. Macdonald noted that when Owen asked Rapp why the Harmonists were changing the site of their social experiment, Rapp replied "in rather a way to avoid the question." Macdonald had already heard, from other sources, that the Harmonists had found Harmonie, Indiana, "unhealthy as well as subject to heat and confined air."

With preliminary conversations about the purchase ended, Robert Owen set off with his party to see the town on the Wabash for himself and to meet the business manager of the Harmonists, Frederick Rapp, who was awaiting him in Indiana. The Owen party bade farewell to their host in Economy and left Pittsburgh in a snowstorm December 6, 1824, on the steamboat *Pennsylvania*. They were at Cincinnati by December 9 and at Louisville the next day. At Louisville, they had to travel two miles downstream by carriage to Shippingport and transfer to the steamboat *Favorite*, because the river was too low for the *Pennsylvania* to go down the Falls of the Ohio. They were at Evansville on December 15. From Evansville there was "a tolerable horse road through the woods" to Harmonie, but the road from Mt. Vernon was shorter and they went on to that town, arriving on the 16th.

After a night at James Inn at Mt. Vernon, the party set off for Harmonie in two wagons, each of which was drawn by four horses. Because the road was rough and the wagons traveled slowly, Macdonald and a companion soon got out and walked, taking a different road, which led them through the Posey County seat of Springfield. There, after noonday dinner at an inn, they were joined in their journey by the innkeeper, one

John Schnee, who was soon to become the postmaster at New Harmony.

Robert Owen, continuing with the wagons, had his first view of Harmonie about a mile from the town at a point where the great forest of oaks, beeches, and tulip and walnut trees opened upon the lands the Württembergers had cleared. Behind the town lay the Wabash River, bordered by forest on its farther shore and disappearing among the trees above and below the village. Vineyards clung to the hills and Indian mounds around the town, and from Owen's eminence he saw that meadows, orchards, and the Harmonist labyrinth skirted the road ahead of him. Looking down thus upon Harmonie, he could count its four streets running north toward the curving river and the six that crossed them and, almost in the center, the open space where the two churches stood, the white wooden church with a steeple and the massive new brick edifice in the shape of a cross. Most of the houses were of logs or clapboarded, and since they were unpainted they had weathered to a dusky slate color; but the bricks of the new church, the dormitories, and some forty houses were bright red. This note of color, plus the order of the streets and gardens, must have been gratifying to the eyes of a man who had seen little besides leafless forests and log cabins for many days.

Frederick Rapp, whom Macdonald described as "a tall, raw-boned, sallow complexioned, serious & plain german," met Owen and his son at the Tavern on Main Street and took them to the top of the Rapp mansion, where they had another good view of the entire village. The next morning, which was warm and rainy with an easterly wind, they went to the top of the new church, from which they had an even better view. After that, they spent the weekend inspecting the town in detail.

Frederick Rapp showed the Owens everything—the mills, the granaries, the greenhouse, the distillery, the brewery, the tannery, the shops, the ropewalk. Most of these enterprises were still in partial operation at least, manned by skeleton crews of the Harmonists who had not yet moved on to Economy. Frederick took his guests to the sheepfolds, the deer park, where they saw "a beautiful elk," the orchards and the vineyards and into the fields. He guided them through the labyrinth and explained the symbolism of the small temple at its center. He entertained them in the Rapp mansion with wine and music, and William Owen became half-enamored of Father Rapp's granddaughter, Gertrude, as she played the piano. He took them to church on Sunday, where about five hundred men and women gathered for the service. And he showed them the footprint stone in the yard of the Rapp house and told them where he bought it and what he believed it was, not the footprints of the Angel Gabriel but the marks left by the bare feet of a prehistoric man.

On Monday, the 20th of December, leaving Robert Owen and Frederick Rapp in Harmonie to discuss their business, Captain Macdonald and William Owen crossed the Wabash and forded Fox Creek beyond it to visit Richard Flower's establishment, known as English Prairie, near Albion in Illinois. But Robert Owen and Frederick and Gertrude Rapp soon joined them and remained with them in Illinois till after Christmas.

When the Owens and the Rapps returned to Harmonie, another busy weekend followed. On Saturday, January 1, 1825, Robert Owen told his son that he had finally made up his mind to purchase the town. On Sunday, January 2, he and Frederick Rapp drew up the terms of the sale. Accounts of the price vary: George Flower said $50,000 was paid for 32,000 acres; Christiana F. Knoedler puts the total at $190,000; Posey County records show Owen paid $125,000 for 20,000 acres a year later. On Monday, January 3, in spite of a letter that came from Morris Birkbeck that morning urging Owen to investigate lands farther west before he closed the bargain, the agreement to purchase Harmonie was signed and sealed, and the town became New Harmony, although many, even the buyers from time to time, continued to refer to it by its old name.

That same afternoon, at three o'clock, restless Robert Owen was off again on his travels. With Captain Macdonald and William Owen he went aboard a keelboat at the New Harmony landing bound for Shawneetown, Illinois, an Ohio River port just below the mouth of the Wabash. It was the first time the party had traveled on a keelboat, and the younger men were much interested in its construction and operation. It was a large open boat with a long cabin in the center about four feet wide and four feet high. The crew was composed of six rowers and a captain, who went below for their supper at sundown and left Captain Macdonald and Robert Owen at the oars and young William at the helm. In spite of his inexperience, William steered in the dark very capably, going aground on a sandbar only once. When the crew returned to their posts, the three passengers ate a meal of cold meat, bread, butter, tea, coffee, milk and sugar that Frederick Rapp had provided for them. Afterward, they curled up in buffalo robes in the unheated cabin for the night.

At Shawneetown, the Owens and Macdonald took passage on the steamboat *Indiana* bound upriver. Their intention was to return to New Harmony and pick up a group of emigrating Harmonists and their goods, but the pilot of the *Indiana* proved unfamiliar with the Wabash and, after advancing into that stream only a short distance, tied up at the shore and sent a messenger ahead to tell the Harmonists to come down and meet them. While they waited, the passengers of the *Indiana* amused themselves by hunting and cutting wood for the boat. They also set fire to several big trees to watch their torchlike burning. This sport was a common pastime of travelers and it was not often discouraged by landowners, because wood ashes were worth more in those days than timber.

Finally, three keelboats came down the Wabash with the Harmonists' goods but with no Harmonists aboard. The Württembergers had either misunderstood their instructions or had preferred to go overland to Mt. Vernon. At any rate, the steamboat was to meet them there. It proceeded then to Mt. Vernon, where Frederick Rapp and a group of his people, mostly women, had spent the night at James Inn. There William and the Captain took leave of the elder Owen, who remained aboard the *Indiana* for the trip East, and after a breakfast at the inn with Mr. Schnee and the county sheriff and a man he had under arrest for a murder in Tennessee, William and the Captain returned to New Harmony.

William and the Captain spent the next few weeks seeing the country roundabout, traveling again into Illinois, and to Princeton and Vincennes in Indiana. After they exhausted the possibilities of travel in the neighborhood, they passed the time from February till April "getting information at Harmonie, conversing with friends, and sometimes pruning trees." William confessed to a great deal of boredom during this period of waiting. He found some entertainment in frequent calls on Gertrude Rapp and her family at the Rapp mansion. In Illinois, at Christmastime, he had decided that Gertrude was "too passive a being"; but in New Harmony he was bored and she was pretty and sang well and always welcomed him. Once, on a warm day in March, he "found Gertrude and her mother ironing, without their jackets." Whether he was shocked or delighted by their deshabille, he did not say; but whatever his emotions, he thought the fact worth noting in his diary. William was twenty-three.

In late March, Frances Wright, the freethinking feminist, and her sister arrived in New Harmony on "palfreys," headed for a rendezvous with General Lafayette in New Orleans. They stayed a day and two nights, and William decided that Frances Wright was "a very learned and fine woman, and though her manners are free and unusual in a female, yet they are pleasing and graceful and she improves upon acquaintance." His friend, Captain Macdonald, remarked of this visit only that "Miss Wright & her sister came here for a day on their way down the river to join La Fayette who is coming up the river in a steamboat in a few weeks. They have lived 5 years with him."

During this period, Macdonald tells us, "Dr. Miller was printing a small pamphlet for Mr. Rapp relative to the Harmonie system. As it was a translation from the German, we assisted him in correcting both the language and the press." This "Dr. Miller" was Johann Christoph Müller, the Harmonist schoolmaster, and the pamphlet was the Rapps' *Gedanken über die Bestimmung des Menschen,* translated as *Thoughts on the Destiny of Man.* William Owen and Captain Macdonald also colored a map of the town that Frederick Rapp gave them. This map, preserved in the Library of the Workingmen's Institute in New Harmony, showed buildings and houses carefully outlined in their exact locations, and the colors William and the Captain applied were red, brown, and blue. They left no key to the coloring of the map, but with only a few discrepancies red seems to represent brick structures and brown either frame or log. In one place, blue is identified as a barn, but this color does not seem to have been used with any consistent plan.

While the two young men were thus occupying their time in Indiana, Robert Owen, having spent eighteen days in the Wabash country and only half of that time in New Harmony itself, was back in the East spreading the gospel of the New Moral World.

14

On Robert Owen's second visit to the nation's capital, Thomas Jefferson, James Madison, and other prominent men in and out of office entertained him. His account of his meetings with these builders of American democracy was that he and his proposal to reform them and their handiwork were received with enthusiasm. On the other hand, the Duke of Saxe-Weimar Eisenach, reporting on his travels through North America in 1825 and 1826, found that "in the eastern states there is a general dislike of him. . . . I heard at that time unfavorable expressions from persons in the highest public offices against him; and one of them gave Mr. Owen to understand very plainly that he considered his intellects rather deranged." Be that as it may, Owen was allowed to speak twice before joint sessions of Congress, with members of the Supreme Court and the Cabinet and the President of the United States himself in attendance, and the American press made generally favorable comments on these speeches.

Before the gatherings in the Hall of the House of Representatives in Washington, Owen exhibited a scale model of the buildings he proposed one day to erect at New Harmony and which he hoped would be copied in many other communities of its kind in the United States. The buildings formed a phalanstery, or hollow square, one thousand feet long by one thousand feet wide, with towered structures at the corners and at the centers of the sides, housing lecture halls, laboratories, a ballroom, a concert hall, a chapel, committee rooms and lounges. The structures forming the rest of the walls were to be family dwellings on the first and second floors and rooms for the unmarried and children over the age of two on the third floors.

Robert Owen
*(The Long Island
Historical Society)*

View of New Lanark
(Indiana State Library)

The phalanstery, as Owen
visualized it

(*Indiana Historical Society Library*)

Robert Dale Owen

(*Indiana State Library*)

Richard Owen

(*Indiana State Library*)

David Dale Owen

(*Indiana Historical Society Library*)

William Owen

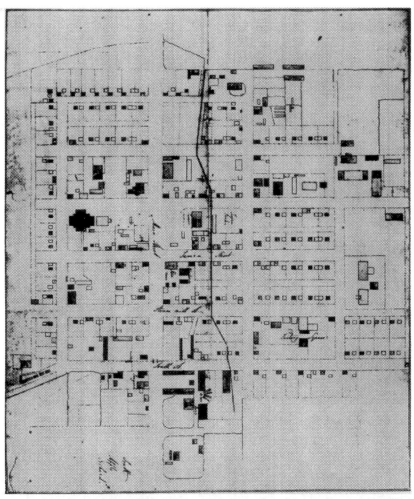

Map of New Harmony, 1825, and a view of the town on the Wabash

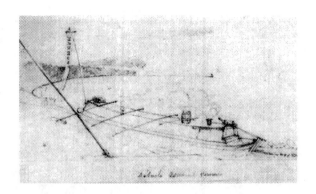

The Boatload of Knowledge, sketched by Charles-Alexandre **Lesueur**
(American Philosophical Society)

Gas, water, and all the conveniences of the times were to be supplied throughout the phalanstery.

As Owen explained it to his audience, his plan was to establish at New Harmony a pattern for lawmakers to follow. He looked forward to the day when the United States would be composed of thousands of small communities with property held in common, such as the one he proposed to build. "If," he conjectured, "these societies spread by their commercial operations, and the increased advantages and comforts which they offer, to the whole population, what effect will they have upon the government and general prosperity of an extensive empire? I . . . reply that a country, however extensive, divided into these arrangements of improved social buildings, gardens, and pleasure grounds, and these occupied and cultivated by people possessing superior dispositions, will be governed with more ease than it can be with the same number of people scattered over the country, living in common villages, towns, and cities under the individual system. . . . Any country will be prosperous in proportion to the number and physical and mental superiority of its people."

Years later, in *Threading My Way,* Owen's oldest son pointed out that his father was "unable to conceive the possibility of ultimate failure in his plans." In his speeches before Congress, Robert Owen certainly demonstrated this blind optimism. He said that after the establishment of his model community at New Harmony "every inclination of the individual or old system of society would break up and soon terminate . . . because it is scarcely to be supposed that any would continue to live under the miserable, anxious, individual system of opposition and counteraction, when they could with ease form themselves into or become members of one of these associations of union, intelligence, and kind feelings."

Shortly after these speeches in Washington, Robert Owen made a blunder from which his plans for New Harmony never recovered; he published a manifesto inviting any and all who were in sympathy with his ideas to go at once to the town on the Wabash and join the community. Of course at this time there was no "community" in New Harmony for them to join and no one there to receive or provide for newcomers except young William and the Lord of the Isles, Captain Macdonald.

The result of this manifesto was that when Robert Owen finally returned to New Harmony, on April 13, 1825, he found awaiting him a horde of people possessing something less than the "superior dispositions" that he had envisaged. There were indeed many on hand with a sincere and earnest wish to form with him a New Moral World. But there was an equal number of crackpots, free-loaders, and adventurers whose presence in the town made success unlikely.

Numbers alone created a major problem. The village was crowded to its full capacity—and of course the last of the German Harmonists had not yet moved out. By the first of June, when Thomas Pears, once employed by Benjamin Bakewell, the Pittsburgh glassmaker, arrived in New Harmony with his wife and seven children ranging in ages from one year to eighteen, the only accommodation available to them was a house with three rooms and a kitchen, a "little tenement," as Mrs. Pears called it, which they had to share with another family.

But Robert Owen was not deterred by these circumstances. He rechristened the Harmonist brick church "The Hall of New Harmony," dedicated it to free thought and free speech, and on April 27 delivered an address in it to the members of his "community" and to the curious who came in from the surrounding country to see what was going on in the once quiet town on the Wabash.

"I am come to this country," he said, "to introduce an entire new state of society; to change it from an ignorant, selfish system to an enlightened social system which shall gradually unite all interests into one, and remove all causes for contests between individuals."

He then repeated the basic principles of his convictions: that man was not a subject for praise or blame but a product of circumstances and that only by changing the circumstances in which he lived could he be redeemed from ignorance and self-ishness. He admitted, however, that these circumstances could not be changed overnight and said that he regarded New Harmony only as "the half way house between the old and the new." For this reason, he said, the people of New Harmony must accept for a while a certain degree of pecuniary inequality, although thenceforth there was to be no social inequality. What was more, this new social order included himself, Robert Owen; for he regarded himself as no better than the lowliest person in his audience. But because no other individual had yet had the same experience as himself in the practice of the new system he intended to introduce, he would have to conduct their affairs for them for a time.

On May 1, 1825, the community adopted the Constitution of the Preliminary Society that Robert Owen had outlined in his address. It is an interesting contrast to the Württembergers' Articles of Association. Where the Harmonists were specific and left no loopholes in their contract, Robert Owen couched his constitution in general language, leaving the practical working out of community problems on an *ad hoc* basis. Where members of the German community pledged themselves to strict obedience to the rules and regulations of George Rapp and his associates and gave up all their property in exchange for a guarantee of food, drink, spiritual guidance, medical care, and such education as Rapp and his associates thought good for them, members of Owen's group were expected to supply their own household goods and tools, invest their capital in the enterprise at interest, and think not in terms of obedience but of independence and the promotion of "the happiness of the world."

Robert Owen's concept of social equality did not extend to "persons of color." This exclusion was made quite clear in the third sentence of the constitution. "Persons of color" might be received into the society "as helpers, if necessary," but if they wanted to contribute to "universal happiness," they were advised to remove themselves from New Harmony and go to Africa for such an experiment, "or in some other country, or in some other part of this country."

Segregation of the races thus preserved, the community was established upon property to be purchased by members of the society or leased or rented to them by Robert Owen, and the society itself was not answerable for its members' debts. All members were to render willingly "their best services for the good of the society, according to their age, experience, and capacity," and in return for these services they were to be given credit at the community store. However, those who did not want to work could buy such credit by paying cash quarterly in advance. Such members, with money of their own and no desire to contribute their services, could also "invest capital on interest" in the community by special arrangement with the governing committee.

Everybody, rich or poor, was expected to be "temperate, regular, and orderly" and to set a good example for everybody else; and if a member's efforts did not produce the happiness he expected from community life, he could leave New Harmony on a week's notice, taking with him, in the products of the establishment, the value of what he had brought, "which value shall be ascertained and fixed by the committee." All members were to have complete liberty of conscience "and be afforded every facility for exercising those practices of religious worship which they may prefer."

The constitution provided only vaguely and loosely for the

government of the society. It stated that Robert Owen "should have the appointment of the committee which is to direct and manage the affairs of the society," and then it went on to define the committee's powers and duties in a single redundant sentence, which stated that the governing committee "would conduct the affairs of the society." Even the size of the governing committee was not defined, beyond the vague proviso that "the number of the committee will be augmented from time to time, according as the proprietor may secure the assistance of other valuable members," and that, at the end of one year, "the members of the society shall elect, by ballot from among themselves, three additional members of the committee."

As soon as this constitution was adopted, Robert Owen exhibited his characteristic impetuosity and optimism. As if the first year of the society's existence had already passed, he announced that he would designate four members of the governing committee and would allow the society, "by ballot among themselves," to elect three more. Among the original committee members, the most noteworthy were Owen's son William; the postmaster, John Schnee, who had moved from Springfield to New Harmony with his family in April; and a versatile gentleman named Robert L. Jennings, who had turned down a good living as a Universalist preacher to become an "Owenite." Jennings later helped William Owen edit the first issues of *The New Harmony Gazette*, served as the equestrian drillmaster of the town's uniformed company of light infantry, and from the pulpit of the Harmonists' frame church confounded the Methodist and Baptist clergymen who came to town and took their turns on that rostrum.

Four days after the adoption of the Constitution of the Preliminary Society, on the morning of May 5, 1825, the *William Penn* tied up at the New Harmony landing. It was one of the four steamboats that were shuttling back and forth between New Harmony and Economy conveying the last of the German

Harmonists and their goods to their new home in Pennsylvania. By two o'clock in the afternoon of that day, the Harmonist cargo was all stowed aboard the *William Penn* and the little steamboat was ready for its passengers. In the meantime, the Harmonists who were to depart on this occasion had gathered in front of the Rapp mansion, where their band played and the women sang farewell hymns.

At three o'clock, having finished this ceremony, the voyagers formed a procession and marched north on Main Street, singing to the music of the band. Where Main Street ended and became the wagon road to the river, they stopped one last time and, turning about, sang a farewell blessing to the town in which they had lived for almost eleven years. After this song, they continued their march toward the boat.

Up to this moment, the ceremonies had been wholly a family affair among the Württembergers. But Robert Owen was following close at their heels and finally, at the river, "caught the opportunity," as Donald Macdonald says in his diary, to make a speech. Robert Owen told the Harmonists then how much he had been impressed by their integrity, justice, and kindness; he said that in all his life he had never met so honest and affectionate a body of people; and he became so moved by his own eloquence "that he could sometimes hardly speak."

After the speech, there was handshaking all around and the little company finally went on board. A gun was fired, and the deck hands cast off the lines. As the steamboat moved downstream, the departing Harmonists and those left on shore waved hats and handkerchiefs while the band played a farewell march. Robert Owen and Captain Macdonald walked back up the river road together, and the Captain says in his diary, "I never in my life returned home after parting with a friend with so sad a feeling as that melancholy afternoon."

In the month that Robert Owen remained in New Harmony

thereafter, many visitors came to the town to hear him speak and to see what was going on. Among them was Morris Birkbeck, a partner of George Flower in Illinois. Already Richard Flower and Owen had fallen out over Owen's refusal to accept Flower's son, George, as a member of his community, but Birkbeck apparently was not involved in this quarrel. Birkbeck had been a frequent visitor in the town since 1817, and his impressions of the contrast between the communities of the Rapps and of the Owens would have been of great value to historians, for in spite of Frederick Rapp's sharp dealing with him he had been reasonably objective in his accounts of the German Harmonists over the eight preceding years. But Birkbeck was never to report what he saw in New Harmony that summer day in 1825; on his way home to Illinois he was drowned while trying to swim on horseback over Fox Creek.

That tragedy happened on June 5, and on the same day Robert Owen again took his leave of New Harmony. After Birkbeck's funeral in the Harmonist cemetery, Owen made a farewell speech to his followers in the Hall of New Harmony and then rode to Mt. Vernon, where he spent the night with Squire J. Y. Welborn. The next morning, while waiting for his steamboat, the *Pioneer,* he "caught" another opportunity to make a speech and addressed an assemblage of forty to fifty people in Mt. Vernon. Captain Macdonald observed that "the meeting broke up without any questions or remarks being made to him."

The *Pioneer* arrived in the afternoon and Owen went aboard, this time accompanied by Macdonald. On this occasion, the founder of the Preliminary Society had spent fifty days in New Harmony, bringing his total time on the scene of his social experiment to less than two months out of the five that had elapsed since his purchase of the town. It would be seven months before he returned. Meantime, William Owen, aged twenty-three, was left behind to keep the experiment in social equality alive while his father arranged his affairs in Scotland and further advertised the community in the eastern part of America.

15

From the beginning, Robert Owen's wife, Caroline, had objected to the American adventure and had done her best to dissuade her husband from undertaking it. When Owen returned to Scotland, sailing with Captain Macdonald from New York on July 16, 1825, and arriving at Liverpool on August 6, he sold his New Lanark interests to obtain funds for completing the purchase of New Harmony and then settled enough money on Caroline Owen to provide for her and the daughters who were to remain in Scotland with her. In return, Mrs. Owen signed away her rights to any share in the New Harmony property, giving her husband a free hand in his operations in America.

Soon after Owen's return to Scotland, Mrs. Owen moved from the countryseat, Braxfield, to Hamilton, near New Lanark, to live in cheaper lodgings. There her daughter Ann died in 1830, she herself died in 1831, and another daughter, Mary, died in 1832. The four sons—Robert Dale, William, David Dale, and Richard—and one of the daughters—Jane Dale—all came to America. Mrs. Owen never saw her sons again, except for a brief visit from Robert Dale, who returned to Scotland once before her death. In her last years she seldom saw her husband.

The Owen mills have survived to the present day and are now operated by The Gourock Ropework Company, Ltd., which manufactures canvas in the New Lanark buildings. One of the gray stone structures in the New Lanark unit on the Clyde was built during Robert Owen's activity there, the millworkers' homes that he remodeled are still there, and the building that housed his school is used today for storage. The two houses in which he and his father-in-law lived in the village remain, but all that survives of Braxfield, the Owen country place nearby, is one vine-covered wall. When a rumor spread in Lanarkshire that the government was going to buy Braxfield and convert it into a public asylum of one sort or another, a neighbor bought it, removed its roof, and allowed it to fall into ruins.

While Robert Owen was in Scotland arranging his financial and family affairs, the Preliminary Society of New Harmony fared reasonably well for a month or two under the impetus of the initial enthusiasm of its members. At the beginning, everyone with serious Utopian ideals lived on the faith that Owen had inspired and in the expectation of his speedy return. Community life was earnest then, but not yet real.

To distract the "Owenites" from reality, there was the stimulus of new acquaintances to be made in the teeming town and new ideas to be exchanged in the long summer evenings when men gathered on the benches in front of the Tavern on Main Street. There was good conversation everywhere, if very little work. As one member of the community wrote, "Here are no brawling braggarts and intemperate idlers . . . here no liquor is sold to inflame the minds of the buyers either at the Tavern or the store, without a certificate from the Doctor that it is needed as a medicine." Since there was only one doctor for the entire community at this time, "certificates" were probably hard to come by.

On Tuesday nights, according to the program Robert Owen proposed before his departure, there was dancing in the Harmonists' brick church, the Hall of New Harmony; on Wednesday nights there was a business meeting with the committee; on Thursday evenings, a concert; and on Sundays, sermons and lectures edified the townspeople in the frame church, some-

times called "the Steeple House." The spirit that prevailed in
the beginning was a spirit of freedom and hope and leisure
and youth. "We have very few *old* men," one member observed.
The average age of the governing committee was somewhere
around thirty. "Still," the observer added, "we are much in
want of farmers, mechanics, and laborers."

The letters of Thomas and Sarah Pears afford the best view,
indeed almost the only view, of the New Harmonists' state of
mind in the early months of the summer of 1825 after Robert
Owen left. These letters were addressed mainly to Benjamin
Bakewell, the Pittsburgh glassmaker, and his wife, who was Mrs.
Pears's aunt. Thomas Pears had once been a partner in the
ownership of a steam grist mill at Henderson, Kentucky, with
John James Audubon, the naturalist, whose wife was a niece
of Benjamin Bakewell. When this enterprise failed, Pears returned to Pittsburgh whence he had come and, afterwards,
went to Europe to bring back glass blowers from France and
England for Bakewell's plant. Pears was living in Pittsburgh
when Owen passed through the city in the winter of 1824. Inspired by Bakewell's enthusiasm for Owenism, he decided at
that time to join the society at New Harmony.

At the outset, Thomas Pears was blindly devoted to the Welsh
social reformer and very optimistic about the success of the
project at New Harmony. "You will perhaps smile at this," he
wrote to Bakewell a few days after his arrival in the town, "but
I have just returned from hearing Mr. Owen, and I am then
always in the hills. I do not know how it is,—he is not an orator;
but here he appears to have the power of managing the feelings
of all to his will. The day before our arrival here, the report of
the committee of which I send you a copy was made public;
and when all found the credit they possessed to be very small,
dissatisfaction prevailed. A day or two after, Mr. Owen spoke,
and it vanished."

The credit to which Pears referred was the maximum of $180

per year that a member of the society could draw upon at the community store for provisions and clothing for his family. A passbook was issued to each member, and in it credits for his labor and debits for whatever he obtained from the store were recorded. There were soon some three hundred of these passbooks in circulation, listing on one page such items as bacon, chickens, eggs, melons, coffee, and hardware, and opposite these entries such credits as plowing, planting, vine culture, storekeeping, carpentering, hatmaking, etc. Women who were not employed by the community were not considered as members and could receive credit in their husbands' passbooks only for such sewing and washing as they were able to do for the society in addition to their own household chores.

William Pelham, who arrived in August and who was, on his arrival, as enthusiastic as Pears had been in June, cited John Schnee as an example of the way a man could live within the community's economic framework if he tried. Schnee was Postmaster, Committeeman, Superintendent of the Farms, and a selling agent for the store. For all these services he was credited with $1.54 a week, and if he wished to take a boarder into his snug little house on Tavern Street opposite the shoe factory, he could add 64 cents more a week to the credit side of his passbook. Schnee had a wife and several sons, two of whom were of working age and could add to the joint credit of the family. Because the Schnees were all "frugal and industrious," Pelham believed they found their allowance "sufficient for their maintenance."

A month or so before Pelham was describing the happy budgeting of the Schnee family, Pears, in one of his letters, was reporting that grumbling had already begun in regard to the passbooks. "The young men," he wrote to Bakewell, "think they, doing as much and paying as much board, ought to have the same credit as their Seniors. The idle and industrious are neither of them satisfied. The one contending that they do enough for their allowance, the other thinking themselves entitled to more. Information is collecting on these heads, and various are the schemes for obviating these sources of dissatisfaction. But I believe that nothing permanent will be determined until Mr. Owen's return."

At the same time, Pears was deploring the lack of order in the town and foresaw no hope for progress until "the Master Spirit" returned. "The hogs have been our Lords and Masters this year in field and garden," he complained. "We are now, as we have been, without vegetables except what we buy; and I believe that we shall go without potatoes, turnips, or cabbages this winter, unless they are purchased."

Hogs and cattle, including horses, were seldom fenced in during Indiana's pioneer period of agriculture. They roamed the woods and fields and towns at random. Maximilian, Prince of Wied, who was in New Harmony in the winter of 1832–1833, reported that "dead swine were lying about in all directions, partly devoured by others." The swine, mostly reddish-brown creatures with round black spots, grew fat on the oak and beech mast in the forest, but they would eat anything else they came upon, except the fruit of the pawpaw tree, which they would not touch, although in Posey County the custard-like pawpaw was—and still is—regarded as a delicacy by some human beings.

Pears's faith in the fundamental assumptions of Owenism had not yet vanished, but he was ready to admit, after three months of observation at first hand, that "the men generally do not work as well as they would for themselves." Even so, even after he lost his job as a bookkeeper in the community store and was on bad terms with the governing committee, he did not waver in his conviction that the return of Robert Owen would set all to rights.

Concurrently, in letters to her aunt in Pittsburgh, Sarah Pears loyally echoed her husband's faith in Owenism, but she was never, like her husband, "in the hills" after being in Robert

Owen's presence. With a practical and critical eye, Sarah Pears looked levelly at the world around her and, womanlike, appraised it in terms of its impact upon herself and her family. In general, the effects of that impact were not auspicious.

For example, the journey from Mt. Vernon to New Harmony got the Pears family off to a bad start. "The roads were terrible, and although the distance is but sixteen miles, it was many days before we recovered from the effects of the ride." And when they reached their destination, the family of nine found themselves assigned to a three-room house and sharing it with a couple named Pearson who had a seven-months-old baby.

Two women do not easily manage one household, but there seemed to be no major disputes between Mrs. Pears and Mrs. Pearson. There was tragedy in the household, however, in a very short while. The Pearson baby died in the house, and to Sarah Pears, mother of a year-old infant herself and fond of children, the death was frightening as well as a sad experience. It was the first death in the community after the Pearses arrived. By summer's end, eight more children had died, and one of them was the five-months-old daughter of Mrs. Pears's closest friend, "the sweetest little creature that I have seen here."

It was a hot, dry summer, with temperatures rising often to 100 degrees and over, and almost everyone in town, afflicted by the heat and dust, suffered from boils and sore eyes. Mrs. Pears complained that her own eyes were in such bad condition that she could not sew. Soon after the Pearses' arrival, their oldest daughter, Maria, caught a bad cold and was unable to shake it off. The community washing to which she was assigned was almost more than she was able to bear, according to her mother. The health of the rest of the family, as Mrs. Pears reported it in her letters, was never better than "indifferent" and "tolerable," and the heat, the mosquitoes, and their cramped and crowded quarters conspired all summer to rob them of their sleep.

"However," Mrs. Pears wrote sharply to her aunt, "to show you the heat is not so great and inconvenient to everyone as it is to me, I must inform you that our balls have never been put off for the most sultry night of the season. The young girls, too, here think as much of dress and beaux as in any place I was ever in."

Her many troubles and exasperations brought Mrs. Pears near the breaking point by mid-November. "It is almost too much for me," she admitted to her aunt in Pittsburgh. "I feel so forlorn that I could say with Cowper, 'I am out of Humanity's reach'. . . . I feel like a bird in a cage shut up forever." At this point her despair was no doubt aggravated by her husband's mood. Of him, in the same letter, she wrote: "Mr. Pears seems very unwilling to write. He is well assured that when Mr. Owen returns all will be well, but at present as he has nothing good to write he prefers to say nothing." Valiantly, but with a degree of cynicism also, the good lady ended her jeremiad with self-recrimination: "But I must try to get out of this dismal strain. I know that I have abundance more than I deserve to be thankful for and will endeavor to look more on the bright side of the picture—if I can find it."

William Pelham fared better in New Harmony than Thomas Pears, possibly because he had a more sanguine temperament to start with, but also because he came to New Harmony alone, troubled by none of the common anxieties of a family man. Pelham arrived on foot from Mt. Vernon in late August, when the worst of the summer heat was over. He had disembarked from the steamboat *Postboy* at Mt. Vernon after a journey down the Ohio from Zanesville. "All the best rooms in the place are occupied," he wrote to his son, William Creese Pelham, the Zanesville postmaster. But after two nights of lodging at the Tavern, he obtained a room in the building where the governing committee were housed. The room was not lathed and plastered and Pelham foresaw that as the cold weather advanced he would have to move "or be frozen to death." So long as the warm days lasted, however, these lodgings were adequate for a single man.

At first, Pelham saw everything in New Harmony in the most favorable light possible, and his enthusiasm did not wane so rapidly, or ever so completely, as did Pears's, although he shared the general sentiment that things would go better after the return of Robert Owen, which was one way of admitting that things were not going so well as they should at the moment. It was Pelham who wrote that "here are no brawling braggarts and intemperate idlers." It was he who reckoned John Schnee's $1.54 a week for his multifarious services sufficient for the maintenance of his family.

At the end of a month in New Harmony, Pelham felt like "an old inhabitant," accounting for his ease in the new surroundings by the fact that he had become acquainted with most of the people in the town and was on good terms with everyone he had met. He had indeed been fortunate in encountering Schnee on his first day in town and being introduced by the postmaster to the most important and influential citizens. "Whatever difference of opinion there may be," Pelham wrote to his son, "(and there is in reality a great difference in religious matters)—I hear no illiberal remarks, I see no overbearing temper exhibited." His only regret was that his son was not in New Harmony to share with him the excitement of the new spiritual and intellectual freedom he was experiencing.

Although Pelham seemed to admire everyone in authority in New Harmony, his highest regard was reserved for Robert L. Jennings, the former Universalist parson. Jennings's oratory seemed to put Pelham in the hills in the same way that Owen's affected Pears. "I have just returned from *Meeting*," he wrote to William Creese Pelham on September 11; "and strange as it may appear to you, I am a *constant attendant*. The orator was

Mr. Jennings; and the substance, and indeed the whole of his discourse was a *moral lecture,* in the plainest and most intelligible language." On another occasion, when the orator introduced Pelham to William Owen, Pelham referred to him as "Rev. Mr. Jennings," and added, "(tell Mr. K he need not be alarmed at this title for Mr. J is truly a minister of rational or natural religion)." He admired Jennings almost equally for his skill in exercising the town's light infantry, saying of him that he was "an excellent disciplinarian, and well acquainted with military tactics."

It was perhaps Jennings more than anyone else who gave the new community a bad name among the pious. His ministry of "rational or natural religion" contributed to the New Harmonists' reputation for atheism, so that by the time Robert Owen eventually returned to America there was a strong body of public opinion opposed to his experiment. Jennings was not content with delivering moral lectures in the old Harmonist church; he delighted also in confuting the sermons of the sectarian preachers who were allowed to use the pulpit under the provisions of the Constitution of the Preliminary Society. On one occasion, Jennings's target was "a rambling shaking quaker" and his "truly christian harangue"; on another, it was a Swedenborgian; on still another, it was the Methodists' preacher, "who sometimes holds forth to the great delight of those who take pleasure in confounding their understanding." But it was in a bout with a Baptist that Jennings incurred the wrath of Christians beyond the limits of the remote little town on the Wabash.

"On Thursday, that is, the next day following my arrival," William Pelham wrote, "a Baptist preacher came into town and announced his intention of delivering a discourse in the evening in the Church. Accordingly, a large congregation assembled, and listened to him with great attention. He is certainly one of their first rate preachers, and he managed his matters with much address. The next evening—(Friday) Mr. Jennings delivered a lecture in the same place, and ably demonstrated the sandy foundation of the ingenious gentleman's arguments, without any pointed allusion to him or his arguments. At the close of the lecture my gentleman thought proper to make a rejoinder, tho nothing had been said of him or his doctrine, but he did not seem to be in so good a humor as he was the evening before—although he had previously performed the marriage ceremony for a young couple—especially when the young couple retired with their friends into the *Hall* to enjoy the pleasures of dancing instead of listening to his rejoinder."

Two months later, Pelham was writing to his son again about this preacher: "The dismal story you copied from the Pittsburgh Mercury was already known here, and the writer is also known. He is a Baptist preacher I heard him preach just after my arrival, and he went away displeased because Mr. Jennings out-preached him. I wd recommend to you to read in the Gazette if you want to know the truth of things—read the 'View of Harmony.' "

It might have been better for the infancy of Owenism in the New World if Jennings had limited himself to reading from the works of Robert Owen and Robert Dale Owen, which was the practice of William Owen when he took his turn in the pulpit. William had a poor speaking voice and was a dull reader. His words in the Steeple House seemed to give no offense anywhere.

Others besides the clergy came to town and went away disenchanted. There were many who could not find accommodations, or who could not endure the accommodations that were assigned to them. There were some who were not admitted at all, because they were too obviously vagrants or their motives were suspect. There were others, like the English ropemaker from Cincinnati who came prepared in advance to be "disappointed and disgusted"; he stayed only a day. And there were still others, like the superintendent of the steam mill who thought his pay was insufficient and who departed disgruntled by the settlement the governing committee made with him. Concerning this man Pelham predicted that, "wherever he goes he will spread a doleful account of the injustice and oppression he experienced at New Harmony and advise his hearers to shun the place as they would a plague or pestilence."

Not all that was said about New Harmony outside its limits was true. Far from it. Even Mrs. Pears, in one of her darkest moments, bridled when she heard about malicious gossip. "I hear that our society bears a very ill name in the neighborhood, and I believe very undeservedly," she wrote to her aunt, in the same letter in which she complained that life in New Harmony was almost too much for her. "There are a few bad members among us, but it seems hard that the whole should suffer for the faults and the follies of the few."

William Pelham's first job in the community was that of accountant in the public store, but from the start he announced a preference for being somehow connected with the printing establishment. Through the efforts of his friend Jennings, this preference was finally realized when the *New Harmony Gazette* was established and began publishing on October 1, 1825. Pelham was at first a general assistant to the editors. He read proof, filed exchanges, and looked after mailing and subscriptions. One of his regular duties was to write a weekly summary of the news, which William Owen or Jennings had to approve. Later, toward the end of the *Gazette's* first year, Pelham was the sole editor of some twenty issues. Within a short while after it began publication, a hundred and twenty-five copies of the *Gazette* were delivered in the town each week (members of the society paid half price, or one dollar per annum, for their subscriptions), and a hundred and seventy-five copies were being sent out to nineteen states of the Union besides Indiana, and to Scotland and England.

THE COMMUNITY OF EQUALITY

The New Harmony Gazette, edited first by William Owen and Robert Jennings and later by Robert Dale Owen and Frances Wright, published regularly every week for three years, until Robert Dale Owen and Miss Wright took it to New York City and renamed it *The Free Enquirer.* It appeared at first on Saturdays and then, after eight issues, on Wednesdays, in quarto, on "fine royal paper." The type was clean and clear, and the impressions made by the brand new Stansbury press that Robert Owen had purchased in the spring in Cincinnati have endured for a century and a half, making the print still legible even where the ink has faded. The motto of the editors was, "If we cannot reconcile all opinions, let us endeavor to unite all hearts"; and they promised that their pages would "ever be open to free expressions of opinions, which, however erroneous, may become useful, where reason and truth are left free to combat them." In all its one hundred and fifty-six numbers the *Gazette* continued to publish contributions that criticized the society as well as essays written in its praise.

Like most newspapers of its time, the *Gazette* contained very little local news other than notices of marriages, deaths, and public meetings. Its pages were often filled with the writings and speeches of Robert Owen; for example, in the first issue Owen's address of the previous April urging the formation of the Preliminary Society was printed in full, and in succeeding issues his *New View of Society,* published in England twelve years before, was serialized in the *Gazette* although bound copies of the treatise were on sale at the New Harmony store for twenty-five cents.

In addition to the previously published writings of Robert Owen, Robert Dale Owen, Frances Wright, William Maclure, and others, the *Gazette* always printed some domestic and foreign news. The rest of its pages were taken up by local notices and fillers on a variety of subjects, such as the fermentation of wine, the removal of warts, rules for polite conversation, and essays on the value of sleep and the virtue of early rising. The author of this latter piece calculated that if a person rose at six o'clock every morning instead of eight, he would, in forty years, gain 29,000 hours out of bed, or three years, one hundred and twenty-one days, and fifteen hours. In one issue there was a poem entitled "Love," followed by an essay on "Lock-Jaw." Articles on the planting of potatoes, the making of sauerkraut, and the cure of asthma were combined in another issue. In the first issue of every month, William Owen's interest in the weather was reflected by charts of meteorological observations that recorded daily temperatures, cloud formations, winds, and precipitation.

The "View of Harmony" that William Pelham recommended to his son was the "View of New Harmony" that William Owen wrote and published in the first and second numbers of the *Gazette*. Young Owen devoted most of the first article to descriptions of the town's buildings and equipment rather than the society's activities and thus paid, unwittingly perhaps, a greater tribute to the "Rappites' " achievements than to the "Owenites'." In almost every department of communal endeavor the author described the potentialities of what the German Harmonists had left behind, but in the second number of the *Gazette* his "View" admitted that their successors had done very little to develop and exploit their inheritance.

For example, adding italics for emphasis:

"With the machinery now in hand, our operations in the wool business should turn out one hundred and sixty pounds of yarn per day, *but the want of spinners reduces the business.*"

"The frilling and dressing departments have, at present, neither regular superintendents nor workmen, *consequently they are not prosecuted with effect.*"

"The cotton-spinning establishment is equal to producing between three and four hundred pounds of yarn per week and is under very good direction, *but skilful and ready hands are much wanting."*

"The dye-house is a spacious brick building, furnished with copper vessels, capable of containing between fifteen hundred and two thousand gallons, and will probably compare in convenience with any in the United States. *At present this valuable establishment is doing nothing for want of a skilful person to undertake the direction of it."*

"The pottery is doing nothing for want of hands."

"We have at present neither saddlers, harness-makers, leather-dressers, coppersmiths, brush-makers, comb-makers, glaziers, nor bookbinders."

The water mill, "capable of turning out sixty barrels of flour in twenty-four hours," and the sawmill, "capable of furnishing an unlimited quantity of lumber," were apparently also idle, since young Owen mentioned their capacities but failed to mention what they were actually producing.

The manufacture of soap, candles, and glue, however, was in full swing, as were the hatmaking and shoemaking departments. That was something. And yet, on reflection, not much. In an overcrowded community where the hogs had eaten all the vegetables and there were not enough houses to go round, flour and lumber were much more important than hats, shoes, and candles. After all, in that climate men and women could go bareheaded—even barefooted, if need be; and the daylight hours were long enough for candles to be regarded as nonessential, even though the *cacoëthes scribendi* in New Harmony was almost as virulent as the mosquito.

Like many of the *Gazette's* subscribers, however, the editor still cherished high hopes for the future; he was sure that with the return of Robert Owen all would be well. To cheer his readers, he published a letter from Robert Owen in the issue of December 14, 1825. It had been written at sea two months earlier while Owen was en route to the United States. It began: "Americans—I am again hastening to your shores and I return with a fixed determination to exert all my powers for your benefit and through you for the world at large."

But by December 14, 1825, when that letter was published in the *Gazette*, Robert Owen had already been on the American shore for six weeks and he had not yet turned up in the Hoosier Zion he had created. What was more, in spite of his "hastening," he was not going to put in an appearance for another month after that letter was published. True, he was busy mustering a company of angels in the eastern states, but in the meantime that old serpent was busy back home in Indiana.

16

Owen arrived at New Harmony on Thursday, January 12, 1826. The weather had been unseasonably warm—up to 78 degrees three days before—and New Harmony was an island surrounded by Wabash floodwaters. He came in the afternoon. According to William Pelham, he was "accompanied only by a Russian lady whom he accidently found somewhere below Steubenville." Donald Macdonald identifies Owen's companion as a "Mrs. Fisher," whom Owen had met in New York in November shortly after his second landing on American soil. According to Macdonald's diary, Robert Owen and Mrs. Fisher, after one discouraging look at the keelboat *Philanthropist* near Pittsburgh, took off for New Harmony together by mail stage. Macdonald does not mention Mrs. Fisher's nationality.

When word of Owen's coming reached New Harmony, a company of schoolchildren and adults tramped through the mire to greet him on the Mt. Vernon road. "All will be well now!" they chanted, and, "He has come back to us!" By seven o'clock that evening he was in the pulpit of the Steeple House once more, making a speech. It was the first of many.

In the course of his remarks that night, Robert Owen told his people that the keelboat *Philanthropist* would soon arrive and in it there would be more learning than was ever before contained in a boat. Thirteen days later, when the vanguard of the *Philanthropist's* passengers reached New Harmony in heavy wagons from Mt. Vernon, they were already labeled for posterity "The Boatload of Knowledge."

The day of their arrival, the 24th of January, was the coldest day of that month; the mud had frozen; the temperature, having dropped eighty-two degrees in two weeks, stood at four below zero. According to Charles-Alexandre Lesueur, whose notes were a mixture of French and English with misspellings in both languages, the *Philanthropist* made its "arrivé à mount Vernon sur les 2 heures," presumably in the afternoon, and William Maclure, Robert Dale Owen, some of the other men, and all the women and children set off the next day for New Harmony with wagons hauling their baggage. On January 26, the keelboat itself, bearing a group of the naturalists who had chosen to stay aboard till the end of the voyage, appeared at the New Harmony landing.

For once, Robert Owen had been accurate in his superlatives: certainly so distinguished a group of men and women had never before made a voyage in a single keelboat. Just how large a load of knowledge was aboard, however, and what was the exact identity of all its components are now difficult to determine; for the *Philanthropist* has become for some descendants of the "Owenites" what the *Mayflower* is to many Americans, and if everybody alleged to have traveled on the boat actually went aboard, it would have sunk at its moorings in Pittsburgh.

The only firsthand reports of the passenger list are those of

Robert Dale Owen, Victor Colin Duclos, Donald Macdonald, and Charles-Alexandre Lesueur, all of whom made the full voyage. Owen and Duclos drew up their lists from memory many years after the journey, and Owen makes no effort to name everyone on the boat while Duclos puts people aboard who were already in New Harmony at the time of its sailing or who came later. Lesueur's notebooks and Macdonald's diary, written on the *Philanthropist,* are the most reliable sources of information, but they do not correspond in all respects. Lesueur, whose spelling of English names is not reliable, accounts for nine men, eight women, ten children, and ten "hommes d'équipage," a total of twenty-seven passengers and ten crewmen. Macdonald mentions nine men, eight women, fifteen children, six boatmen, and a captain—or thirty-two passengers and seven crewmen.

With almost absolute certainty it can be said that the following were aboard during most of the voyage:

William Maclure, the geologist and philanthropist, who had decided to invest $150,000 in the New Harmony venture and who had the keelboat built at Pittsburgh for the voyage;

Robert Dale Owen, this time making the journey to America with his father;

Thomas Say, zoologist, conchologist, descriptive entomologist, Curator of the American Philosophical Society, and Professor of Natural History at the University of Pennsylvania;

Charles-Alexandre Lesueur, who was later famous for his classification of the fishes of the Great Lakes and became the first Curator of the Museum of Natural History of Le Havre, France, and who, before that, was to send back to France from New Harmony what his French biographer describes as "un *pool-cat,* un skung qui n'a encore jamais été vu vivant en Europe";

Guillaume Sylvan Casimir Phiquepal d'Arusmont, an undisciplined disciplinarian of the schoolroom, in Maclure's employ, who went by the name of William S. Phiquepal in America but who later, when he became the husband of Frances Wright, resumed his full monicker, perhaps simply to preserve his identity;

Madame Marie Louise Duclos Fretageot, the Philadelphia schoolmistress from Paris, who boarded the boat with Maclure at Wheeling after traveling from Pittsburgh with him by coach;

Madame Fretageot's twelve-year-old son, Achille, later variously nicknamed "Sheel" and "Kill" by New Harmonists, according to their linguistic backgrounds;

Dr. Samuel Chase, a chemist, and his wife, who was an artist and musician of sorts and who later married Richard Owen;

Dr. William Price (not to be confused with his younger brother, Dr. Philip Price, who was already in New Harmony lecturing on the circulation of the blood) and his wife and three children;

A young Swiss artist known as Balthazar, whose last name was variously spelled but was probably Obeonesser;

John Beal, a New York Quaker, and his wife and infant daughter, Caroline;

Miss Lucy Sistaire, who would later marry Thomas Say, and her two sisters (all charges of Madame Fretageot);

Miss Virginia Poullard Dupalais, a member of Lesueur's party, and her brother Victor;

Cecelia Noël from Santo Domingo, Lesueur's ward, who later married Achille Fretageot;

Peter and Victor Duclos, students.

Possibly on the boat were Cornelius Tiebout, an engraver, and his daughter, Caroline, a student, and John Speakman and his family. Speakman was a friend of Thomas Say's and one of the founders of the Philadelphia Academy of Natural Sciences. He had operated an apothecary shop at the corner of Second and Market Streets in Philadelphia. Later, in New Harmony, he and his wife named a daughter Indiana.

Macdonald lists a "Miss Turner" aboard the keelboat, as does Lesueur, who writes "Saly" after the name. Later, Lesueur writes "Saly" as "Miss Sale," which some historians have mistakenly transcribed as "Miss Hale," thus creating an extra, non-existent passenger on the boat. Finally, Robert Owen's man-servant, a Mr. Smith, was one of the "Boatload." He helped with the cooking and the chores and was perhaps counted among the crew. Definitely not on the *Philanthropist,* although several authorities have listed him among the passengers, was Gerard Troost, the Dutch geologist. Troost came to New Harmony at least a month before the keelboat's arrival.

Most of the *Philanthropist's* passengers boarded at Pittsburgh on December 8, 1825. A month later, when Donald Macdonald arrived at Pittsburgh from Washington, where, as Owen's agent, he had presented to the President of the United States an architect's model of the New Harmony-to-be, he expected to buy passage on a steamboat that would either overtake the *Philanthropist* on the Ohio River or arrive at Mt. Vernon close upon the keelboat's wake. To his amazement, however, he found not only that all steamboats at Pittsburgh had been driven high on shore by the frozen river but learned also that the *Philanthropist,* with his friends aboard, was still only thirty miles downstream. Pushed into the woods by the ice coming down the river, it had been stuck there for a whole month, near Beaver, Pennsylvania, just below George Rapp's new village of Economy.

Although Maclure and Madame Fretageot and Robert Owen and the mysterious "Mrs. Fisher" had impatiently chosen to proceed overland, the rest of the passengers regarded the delay in the ice-locked woods as a holiday. Young Robert Dale Owen, who had read James Fenimore Cooper's *The Pioneers* in England, was now seeing the world of Natty Bumppo at first hand

and was improving his time by learning woodcraft. The ladies and the children were skating, and two little French boys had already fallen through the ice without serious consequences. The men were providing the *Philanthropist's* table with fresh game every day, and one of these hunters had broken a leg falling over a rail fence. The naturalists on the boat—Say and Lesueur especially—were in their proper element, and by the time Macdonald arrived they had decorated the walls of the men's apartments in the cabin with stuffed fish and birds and a stuffed brown fox, all destined for the museum at New Harmony. In the roomy cabin of the keelboat there were apartments for the men, for the crew, for the ladies, and for the children. The gentlemen had already gallantly christened the ladies' quarters "Paradise." In Lesueur's diagram, the children's apartment, at the stern, is labeled "Purgatoire."

The day of Captain Macdonald's arrival, January 8, was employed cutting a channel through the ice back to the river, which had at last opened. It was strenuous work and everyone lent a hand, but Charles-Alexandre Lesueur found time to make some vivid sketches of the operation, which are still preserved in the Museum of Natural History of Le Havre. The next day, January 9, the *Philanthropist* recommenced its journey, traveling at the rate of five miles an hour, with the male passengers spelling the crew at the sweeps. At night, if the wind was high, the keelboat tied up to the shore; but if the water was calm and the current not too strong, the captain let the boat drift downstream at two miles an hour with the oars unmanned.

The daily exercise of rowing was healthful and agreeable for the men, and for the ladies and the men off duty there was never an end to the variety of scenery that glided past on either side. Periodically there were greetings from the log cabins, frame houses, and occasional brick homes that studded the shores and salutes to the long narrow pennant that unfurled bravely in the wind from the boat's masthead revealing the word "Philanthropist" to one side of the river and "Harmony" to the other. The naturalists busied themselves observing birds and animals and collecting specimens. Lesueur records, in his melange of English and French, long lists of creatures that include a "bald aigle," a "blue geai," a "tukey buzard," and "le cardinal."

Settlers supplied the voyagers with milk, eggs, poultry, and sometimes fruit, and daily the hunters went ashore in the skiff and brought back game. The weather was frosty and invigorating, and the cabin was snug and warm, heated by two large wood stoves and a stone fireplace. At night the passengers conversed and read or watched the naturalists stuff and mount their specimens. Once or twice, when the weather was mild enough and the moon was up, everybody went out and sat atop the cabin and sang.

To break the close confinement aboard the *Philanthropist,* there were frequent stops for visits in the houses along the shores and for shopping in the towns, at Wheeling and Steubenville and Cincinnati and Louisville. Below Wheeling, which Lesueur spells "Willing," there was an "écho remarquable," and everyone appeared on the deck of the "quilleboat" to hear his voice recorded by the river. At Steubenville, a judge came aboard and placed his ten-year-old son in the care of the passengers for schooling at New Harmony and paid twenty-five dollars in advance for the first quarter of his term. At Wheeling, William Maclure and Madame Fretageot joined the party. On the night of January 18, above Madison, Indiana, the keelboat was rocked by the passing of several steamboats "avec une rapidité étonnante," among them the *Bolivar,* which the *Philanthropist* had left behind at the Pittsburgh wharf. At Louisville, Joseph Neef, Maclure's first Pestalozzian teacher in Philadelphia, visited the boat with one of his daughters and promised to sell his farm and join the community on the Wabash in the spring. Below Louisville, everyone remained on deck to watch the spectacle of shooting the Falls of the Ohio.

This troop of brilliant, eccentric, and lighthearted people aboard the *Philanthropist* had been recruited by Robert Owen in the eastern states in spite of frequent pleas by his son, William, that he bring no more disciples to the overcrowded town. By the time they arrived, New Harmony already had a population of one thousand, and what the town needed most, as William had written to his father as soon as he landed in New York, was mechanics and laborers, even though, as William warned at the same time, "We have no room for them." The assemblage of intellectuals on the *Philanthropist* was going to be an economic burden in New Harmony, to say the least. And yet if "The Boatload of Knowledge" had not come to New Harmony, Robert Owen's social experiment in America would have received a much smaller place in history and the "Golden Age" of cultural achievements in the village on the Wabash during the next fifty years would probably not have been realized. Certainly the gaiety and charming irresponsibility of New Harmony in the very midst of the society's collapse during the next few months after the *Philanthropist's* arrival would have been missing. These thirty or so people were babes in the woods, beguiling in their innocence and enthusiasm, delightful even in their subsequent quarrels.

Robert Dale Owen, for example, found everything "wonderfully pleasant" in New Harmony at once and plunged into the new life with zest. At this time, according to his autobiography, he had too much of his father's "all-believing disposition to anticipate results which any shrewd, cool-headed business man might have predicted." Robert Dale Owen was young, only twenty-four, and although the accommodations in the town were crude and the fare simple he was untroubled by hardships. Inspired by the good fellowship and the absence of conventionalism, he entered into the spirit of communal living and undertook any job that needed doing. He helped tear down dusty and dilapidated log cabins; he sowed wheat for a day and got a sore arm; after that, he tried helping with the community baking and ruined the bread. Eventually, he settled down to schoolteaching and editing the *Gazette,* endeavors more in keeping with his talents, his training, and his physique.

Young Owen was popular with the eccentrics of the town because their ways delighted him. He was especially amused by an old man named Greenwood, father of Miles Greenwood, who would later become Chief of the Cincinnati Fire Department. When there were thunderstorms—and thunderstorms are frequent in New Harmony—the elder Mr. Greenwood would walk through the streets carrying an iron rod ten or twelve feet long. When Owen asked him why he did this, Greenwood explained that he was very old and wanted to die but felt he had no right to kill himself; he hoped the Lord would take care of his problem with a bolt of lightning.

Another favorite of Owen's was Professor Joseph Neef, a veteran of the Napoleonic wars. Neef was a kindly man, but his pupils in New Harmony's Pestalozzian school were often afraid of him because of his soldier's profanity. Once when Neef heard a boy swear and chided him for it, the boy said, "But why do you swear, Professor Neef?" "Because I am a damn fool, boy!" the old soldier said. "But don't you be one too."

The one person whose eccentricities Robert Dale Owen could not abide was Guillaume Sylvan Casimir Phiquepal d'Arusmont. He regarded Phiquepal as a "wrong-headed genius" and thought his unforgivable conceit destroyed his usefulness in the school. Like his father, Robert Dale Owen considered pedagogy the very basis of reform and his enthusiasm for people did not extend to those who stood in the way of success for the social experiment.

The school at New Harmony, in spite of the solemn theories

and high principles of its founders and teachers, had its lively moments, at least for the pupils. Years later, Mrs. Sarah Cox Thrall recalled the dormitory life in Community House No. 2:

"We went to bed at sundown in little bunks suspended in rows by cords from the ceiling. Sometimes one of the children at the end of the row would swing back her cradle, and, when it collided on the return bound with the next bunk, it set the whole row bumping together. This was a favorite diversion, and caused the teachers much distress. At regular intervals we used to be marched to the community apothecary shop, where a dose that tasted like sulphur was impartially dealt out to each pupil, just as in Squeers' Dotheboys school. Children regularly in the boarding-school were not allowed to see their parents, except at rare intervals. I saw my father and mother twice in two years. We had a little song we used to sing:

> "Number 2 pigs locked up in a pen,
> When they get out, it's now and then;
> When they get out, they sneak about,
> For fear old Neef will find them out."

Victor Colin Duclos, who was on "The Boatload of Knowledge," put his recollections of schooldays in New Harmony on paper seventy-five years after the long voyage from Pittsburgh. He recalled that Thomas Say and Charles-Alexander Lesueur spent much of their time searching for shells and catching fish, which they described and painted, but that Lesueur also painted sets for theatrical productions in the Hall of New Harmony. Lesueur was clean-shaved when he left Philadelphia but he grew a beard in New Harmony. This he plaited and tucked inside his coat when he was working out of doors, followed about by his three dogs, Penny, Snap, and Butcher. Lesueur made New Harmony his home for eleven years, from 1826 until

1837, when he returned to France. He died in Le Havre in 1846.

According to Duclos, Thomas Say was the boys' favorite teacher, while the Swiss painter called Balthazar had the hardest time at their hands. When Balthazar produced a picture of the "Rappite" church, the boys decided the lines were not perpendicular and painted poles propping up one side and men with ropes trying to pull the other side straight. On another occasion, when Balthazar quarreled with a man named Mike Craddock and challenged him to a duel, the boys loaded the pistols with powder only. Craddock, in on the secret, dropped "dead" at the first fire, and Balthazar, terrified, began to cry, "For God's sake, run for a doctor!" Balthazar was so sensitive to the teasing that followed this affair of honor that he soon returned to Europe, announcing that he wished to return to "the company of gentlemen."

No doubt the happiest occasions for schoolboys in those days were the times when fire broke out in the town. Then the old fire engine that the German Harmonists had left behind would be dragged out by its crew of eighteen men. The fire engine was built for the Harmonists in 1804 in Philadelphia and was named affectionately for its manufacturer, "the Pat Lyons." It was still in occasional use in New Harmony a century later.

The Duke of Saxe-Weimar Eisenach visited New Harmony in April, 1826, and although he had grave doubts about the success of Robert Owen's ideas in practice, he succumbed to the charm of the town's inhabitants. Soon after he arrived, he met in the Tavern "a man, very plainly dressed, about fifty years of age, of rather low stature," and after conversation with him about the disorder of the place, he was surprised to learn that his new acquaintance was Robert Owen. Owen introduced the Duke to his sons and to Maclure, who had moved into the Rapp mansion, and gave him a guided tour of the town. That evening the Duke heard a concert by a "surprisingly good" or-

"Rappite" frame and brick churches, sketched by Lesueur, 1826

David Dale Owen's sketch of Steeple House and Hall of New Harmony, 1830

Lesueur's sketches of Church Street and Hall of New Harmony

Thespian Society theatre ticket
(Indiana Historical Society Library)

"Rappite" schoolhouse and
Dormitory No. 1, by David
Dale Owen
(Indiana State Library)

Lesueur's drawing of the Hall of
New Harmony and his house,
1831
(American Antiquarian Society)

View from doorway of the Hall,
by Lesueur
(Muséum d'Histoire Naturelle du Havre)

Charles-Alexandre Lesueur,
drawn by Karl Bodmer
(*American Antiquarian Society*)

New Harmony in 1832,
watercolor by Karl Bodmer
(© *Northern Natural
Gas Company,
Joslyn Art Museum*)

Charles-Alexandre Lesueur,
watercolor by Karl Bodmer
(© *Northern Natural
Gas Company,
Joslyn Art Museum*)

William Maclure

Frances Wright, 1826, in the costume of the Community of Equality

(Indiana State Library)

Madame Marie Duclos Fretageot

(Indiana State Library)

Thomas Say

Joseph Neef

chestra and was impressed by a recitation of Byron's poetry by Robert Jennings.

The Duke learned that most of the young girls in New Harmony plaited straw hats in their homes to help with the family credit in the town store, but in spite of this manual labor they kept themselves apart from the common people at lectures and dances. Madame Fretageot confided, in German, that she was irked by the equality Mr. Owen insisted upon, and the Duke noticed that at dances she kept the young ladies "of the better class" under her protection in a corner. The Duke also noted that Thomas Say, always in delicate health, partly because he half-starved himself on a diet that William Maclure also observed, had badly blistered hands from the unaccustomed labor he performed. Say struck the German as a comical figure in the costume that Owen had prescribed for the community—"white pantaloons, buttoned over a boy's jacket, made of a light material, without a collar."

Sarah Pears took a much more lugubrious view of this costume and of the dress prescribed for women. "The female dress," she wrote back to Pittsburgh, "is a pair of undertrousers tied round the ankles over which is an exceedingly full slip reaching to the knees, though some have been so extravagant as to make them rather longer, and also to have the sleeves long. I do not know whether I can describe the men's apparel but I will try. The pantaloons are extremely full, also tied around the waist with a very broad belt, which gives it the appearance of being all in one. A fat person dressed in the elegant costume I have heard very appropriately compared to a feather bed tied in the middle. They are tied around the neck like the girls' slips, and as many wear them with no collars visible, it is rather difficult to distinguish the gentlemen from the ladies. When I first saw the men with their bare necks it immediately struck me how very suitable they were equipped for the executioner."

Perhaps it was because these babes in the woods were so ludicrous in their "Owenite" dress that the serpent paused a little while to enjoy the spectacle before he finally struck.

17

When Robert Owen made his third visit to New Harmony, in January, 1826, after an absence of seven months, he had reached a point in his life from which he would thereafter never retreat, a point where, for him, the truth was only what he wanted to believe and facts were of no importance. Whatever the cause, he either ignored the chaos to which he was returning in Indiana or was unaware of it and, on January 25, without waiting for the *Philanthropist* to reach the New Harmony landing, announced that he was so pleased with the progress the community had made in his absence that he wanted the inhabitants to leave the "half-way house" of the Preliminary Society and to organize at once, two years ahead of schedule, a permanent community of equality based on the principle of common property.

Robert Dale Owen, the son, had been in town less than twenty-four hours when his father told him what he proposed to do. The son was not yet oriented to his new surroundings. Indeed he was still blinded by enthusiasm for the theory of socialism without much experience of its practice. Moreover, he had fallen in love with New Harmony the moment he first saw it. And yet what his father proposed took the young man by surprise, and in spite of his youth he was wise enough to see that the decision was hasty.

The meeting that Robert Owen addressed on January 25 resolved itself into a constitutional convention, with Dr. Philip Price as President and Thomas Pears as Secretary; and a committee was thereupon elected to draft the constitution. This committee was composed of Warner W. Lewis, who had been Secretary of the Preliminary Society; Judge James O. Wattles, William Owen, and Robert L. Jennings, all of whom had been members of the governing committee of the Preliminary Society; and Robert Dale Owen and Donald Macdonald, both just up from Mt. Vernon where they had disembarked from the *Philanthropist*. Among others who received votes in the balloting but were not elected were William Maclure, William Pelham, Thomas Say, and the most unlikely of candidates, Guillaume Sylvan Casimir Phiquepal d'Arusmont, who got four votes.

On February 1, 1826, the committee made its report, and after six sessions of debate the constitution was adopted on February 5. The official name of the permanent society was to be The New Harmony Community of Equality. In a preamble, the constitution declared that the object of the community was "that of all sentient beings, happiness." Its principles were:

"Equality of rights, uninfluenced by sex or condition, in all adults.

"Equality of duties, modified by physical and mental conformation.

"Cooperative union, in the business and amusements of life.

"Community of property.

"Freedom of speech and action.

"Sincerity in all our proceedings.

"Kindness in all our actions.

"Courtesy in all our intercourse.

"Order in all our arrangements.

"Preservation of health.

"Acquisition of knowledge.

"The practice of economy, or of producing and using the best of everything in the most beneficial manner.

"Obedience to the laws of the country in which we live."

The preamble continued with a list of conclusions that the society regarded as self-evident and others that its members had arrived at through experience. Among those that were self-evident were the beliefs that freedom was the inalienable right of every human being and that the preservation of life in its most perfect state is the first of all practical considerations. From "experience" the founding fathers derived the same principles that Robert Owen had arrived at years before and had cherished unaltered ever since. "Man's character," the constitution stated, echoing Owen, "is not of his own formation, and . . . artificial rewards and punishments are equally inapplicable: kindness is the only consistent mode of treatment and courtesy the only rational species of deportment." Kindness, courtesy, cooperative union, order and economy, self-knowledge and truth, therefore, were to be the order of the day.

Getting down to the practical business of self-government, the constitution divided the community into six departments:

Agriculture
Manufactures and Mechanics
Literature, Science, and Education
Domestic Economy
General Economy
Commerce

Each of these departments was to have a Superintendent, nominated by the members of the society who were engaged in the occupations involved, and confirmed by the assembly of all members of the society. The Superintendent of the Department of Commerce would be the ex officio Treasurer of the whole society, and the Superintendent of the Department of Domestic Economy would likewise become the society's Commissary. These two, plus an elected Secretary of the society and the four other departmental superintendents, would form the Council of the society, in which was vested the executive power. Laws were to be made by the assembly of "all the resident members of the Society above the age of twenty-one years, one sixth of whom shall be necessary to constitute a quorum for the transaction of business."

No person could be admitted to membership in the community without the consent of the majority of *all* the members of the assembly, and no member could be dismissed from the society except by a vote of two-thirds of the membership. On the other hand, each member had the right of resignation on one week's notice, and when a member resigned or was dismissed from the community, the Council, "subject to an appeal to the assembly," was to determine his compensation for services to the community.

Money brought into the community by members was to be returned to them on withdrawal from the society. But the society was not responsible for individual debts contracted by members. The constitution could be altered only by a vote of three-fourths of the members of the assembly, and then only after four successive public discussions held in four consecutive weeks.

Writing about this constitution years later, Robert Dale Owen called it "liberty, equality, and fraternity in downright earnest. . . . It found favor with that heterogeneous collection of radicals, enthusiastic devotees to principle, honest latitudinarians, and lazy theorists, with a sprinkling of unprincipled sharpers thrown in."

Eleven days after the adoption of the constitution, Thomas Pears was writing home to Pittsburgh: "For my own part I like the System but am completely out of humor with the practice here."

William Pelham, as usual, was more at ease. To Zanesville he was writing, about the same time as Pears's letter: "During the last 8 months the want of organization and arrangement has caused much perplexity and difficulty, and the introduction now of order and regularity into the several departments will be comparatively easy. I anticipate that in 6 months the New Harmony machine will go like a piece of clockwork."

Sarah Pears again took a personal view of the world about her, and it was a dim view. To her uncle she wrote: "Oh, if you could see some of the rough uncouth creatures here, I think you would find it rather hard to look upon them exactly in the light of brothers and sisters. Mr. Owen says we have been speaking falsehoods all our lives, and that here only we shall be enabled to speak the truth. I am sure that I cannot in sincerity look upon these as my equals, and that if I must appear to do it, I cannot either act or speak the truth. . . . I think that the person who wrote that this is a terrestrial paradise must have very odd ideas of paradise, or it must be meant as a joke."

As for Captain Donald Macdonald, he made no comment; he simply wrote in his diary, "I left New Harmony on March 4." He never returned.

Less than two weeks after "the permanent community" was formed, the town's affairs had become so chaotic that the Council unanimously asked Robert Owen to take back what he had given them. The members of the Council at that time were:

Dr. Philip Price, Agriculture
Joseph K. Coolidge, Manufactures and Mechanics
Thomas Say, Literature, Science, and Education
Stedman Whitwell (an architect who had come from England on the ship with Owen), General Economy
William Owen, Commerce, the Treasurer
Richeson Whitby (soon to leave for Nashoba with Frances Wright and marry her sister), Domestic Economy, the Commissary
Warner W. Lewis, the Secretary

Complying with the Council's request, Robert Owen assumed the directorship of the society for one year. Thomas Pears referred to the new government as an "aristocracy," but

Mrs. Pears called it a "dictatorship." Whatever it was, some order came back into the government for a while, but many members were disgruntled and left town, accusing Owen of going back on his promise to turn over the entire property to the inhabitants. Already one separate community had been organized, breaking off from the parent society, and soon another was to follow.

The first of these splinter societies called itself Macluria. Situated on a stretch of land to the north and east of New Harmony on the north side of the Evansville-and-Princeton Road and, beyond its fork, along the Princeton Road, Macluria was led for a few weeks by Donald Macdonald until his departure from New Harmony; it was composed of members of the Preliminary Society who found Owen's views on religion unpalatable. Macluria modeled its constitution, however, on the constitution of the parent society, although it denied women the privilege of voting and put emphasis on age rather than youth. The executive authority was lodged in "The Council of Fathers," composed of the five oldest male members of the group under the age of sixty-five.

The second offshoot of the society was the work of English farmers who had come from English Prairie, in Illinois, after the death of Morris Birkbeck. They too objected to the religious latitudinarianism of Owen. Their government was similar to that of Macluria, although they set the top age for their Council at fifty-five, instead of sixty-five, and insisted that three of its members "shall be good practical agriculturists." This community, east and southeast of New Harmony, was organized early in March, 1826, and called itself Feiba Peveli.

Stedman Whitwell, the English architect, was responsible for the name. Troubled by the repetition of place names in the world, especially in America where Washingtons and Springfields abound, for example, Whitwell devised a scheme of nomenclature based on the latitude and longitude of places and designed to identify immediately their locations. His plan was described at length in *The New Harmony Gazette* for April 12, 1826, with a table of interchangeable vowel and consonant substitutes for the numerals in latitudes and longitudes, as follows:

	1	2	3	4	5	6	7	8	9	0
Vowel Substitutes	a	e	i	o	u	y	ee	ei	ie	ou
Consonant Substitutes	b	d	f	k	l	m	n	p	r	t

Had Mr. Whitwell's suggestions for the use of this table met with success beyond the region in which it was invented, New York City would today be Otke Notive, our Federal Government would have its seat in Feili Nyvul, the people of Pittsburgh would be struggling with the pronunciation of Otfu Veitoup, and lovers of Paris would be dreaming of Oput Tedou in the springtime.

Fortunately for the printers and readers of maps, New Harmony was never rechristened Ipba Venul, as Mr. Whitwell suggested, and Feiba Peveli itself has lost its identity and is once more a part of the parent town. A third offshoot of the community was known simply as Community No. 4. A fifth, in which Owenism died before it was born, might indeed have fared better if it had been christened with one of Mr. Whitwell's concoctions, for today the only way to locate the land Robert Owen deeded for it is to say that it lies halfway between New Harmony and a Posey County settlement called Bugtown, which was formerly listed by the U.S. Post Office as Rapture.

18

The peace that followed Robert Owen's assumption of the directorship of the Community of Equality in mid-February, 1826, was short-lived. Already Macluria had been formed by dissenters. Feiba Peveli came into existence soon after. By March 4, Donald Macdonald was leaving town in silent disillusion, and he was only one of a general exodus of unhappy communists at that time.

This exodus might have relieved the strain on the overcrowded village and made Owen's brand of communism ultimately more practicable, but unfortunately new residents came in as old residents departed. Among the newcomers, two are worthy of note: Paul Brown, because he was articulate and left a record of his twelve months in New Harmony, and William Taylor, because he contributed to the collapse of New Harmony's morale by outsmarting Owen in a business transaction. There were many others like Brown and Taylor in temperament and conduct.

Paul Brown had a chip on his shoulder from the start, and what he wrote about Owen and New Harmony must be taken with a grain of salt. Before he arrived in New Harmony on April 2, 1826, he was already prepared to think the Owens would not appreciate his virtues, for he had written two letters of inquiry about the community to them and got no replies. Immediately upon his arrival he found the place "anything but tranquil." This observation was certainly correct; but lacking William Pelham's open heart and Thomas Pears's continuing faith when in the presence of adversity, Brown perversely enjoyed seeing things in their worst light.

The contrast between the conclusions that Brown and the Duke of Saxe-Weimar Eisenach simultaneously drew from the same set of circumstances will serve to illustrate Brown's approach to facts. The Duke, arriving in New Harmony about a week after Brown, observed that William Maclure occupied the Rapp mansion, the finest house in town, while "Mr. Owen, on the contrary, contented himself with a small apartment in the tavern." Brown, contemplating Owen's choice of quarters, found a different basis for comparison. "A great part of the time people were very much stinted in their allowances of coffee and tea, butter, milk, etc.," he wrote. "Mr. Owen, constantly boarding at the tavern where luxurious regale was copiously provided to sell to traveling men and loungers, for money, drank rich coffee and tea."

Brown was angry with the *Gazette* because it did not publish his letters nor report his lectures in the Steeple House, although the newspaper did indeed give an account of one of them. In it Brown criticized the community for its "vain and trifling" amusements and condemned playing cards because they were "invented expressly for the diversion of a weak-minded monarch, to amuse his vacant hours." He was also angry with Robert Owen, who in turn became angry with him for his constant grumbling in public. "Because you are poor," Brown quotes Owen as saying to him on one occasion, "you want those who have wealth to make common property."

That was exactly what Brown wanted. Owen's failure to give his property to the members of the community was the basis of Brown's grudge against the reformer. "The whole course of his practice and preaching," Brown wrote later, "had a bad effect upon the morals of the place. His practice tended to inspire cupidity, and his preaching tended to inspire apathy or licentiousness." Brown accused Owen of establishing a kind of feudal barony. In the book that he published in Cincinnati after he left New Harmony, he remarked, "To talk of common property . . . to a set of people that did not own an inch of the ground on which they lived, that were liable to be expelled at every moment . . . was just as wise as if one of our southern planters should preach such doctrines to his community of black citizens."

Brown said the farmers on New Harmony lands were spiritless and discouraged and the people in the town strangers to each other. He saw weeds all around him "as high as houses," holes in fences, and swine, cows, and horses ranging in the gardens. He complained that shirts, handkerchiefs, and stockings were constantly stolen from the boarding-house laundries and that pilfering prevailed generally in the town. He accused New Harmony mothers of letting their children run wild and said that on one occasion he saw two women fighting with their fists outside Community House No. 4.

Brown finally drew up his own constitution for the community and proposed to read it at a public meeting, but Robert Owen, he said, tore down all the notices. After that, he and others planned and organized a mock funeral for the social system, but somebody—he does not say who—broke into the armory and smashed the coffin they had built for the ceremony. When finally Brown left town, he ridiculed Owen's assertion that the social system was firmly established, pointing out that the tavern charged three dollars a week for board, the store was owned by an individual, a cotton mill was owned by an individual, a distillery was owned by an individual, and Robert Owen himself owned most of the houses and leased them to individuals.

The individual who owned the distillery was William Taylor. He came to town about the same time as Brown; but he did not come with a chip on his shoulder; he came smiling and professing to be an ardent disciple of Owen and a confirmed believer in the system; and in a very short while he was in business with Robert Henry Fauntleroy, with William Owen as a silent partner, operating the community store. When the partnership was ultimately dissolved and an advertisement of its dissolution was published in the *Gazette*, Robert Owen deeded to Taylor about 1,500 acres of land two and a half miles northeast of New Harmony on either side of the Princeton Road for the establishment of a community. The legend is that Taylor was to have the land "with all thereon" and the night before it came into his possession he moved onto it all the livestock and tools he could find in the neighborhood. Taylor immediately set up a distillery on this land, embarrassing Owen, who had prohibited the sale of liquor in New Harmony. The proposed "community" was a swindle.

In the pages of the *Gazette* the dissensions that were tearing New Harmony asunder went unnoticed. The newspaper continued to print the speeches and writings of Robert Owen; the feature for the spring of 1826 was a serialized reprint of two long orations he had delivered in Dublin three years before. The *Gazette* ran an abstract of the proceedings of the constitutional convention and published the "permanent" constitution the community had arrived at. It reprinted several essays by William Maclure, which he had originally written in 1819 for the *Revue Encyclopédique* and which had been rejected by the French censors. It announced lectures by William Ludlow on "Happiness" and other subjects and advertised a course of lectures by Gerard Troost on mineralogy. It explained a "Divital Invention" that Constantine Samuel Rafinesque, Ph.D., of Louisville, had patented to eliminate the use of money as a medium of exchange. And it told its readers how to remove corns and cultivate the grape. But it gave them no hint that Owenism was in a parlous state; in fact, from its glowing reports of other Owenite communities springing up roundabout —one of them at Blue Springs, near Bloomington, Indiana— the *Gazette's* readers might have concluded that Owen's predictions to the Congress of the United States a year before were coming true.

Meantime, Owen himself continued to assure his flock serenely that the New Jerusalem was at hand, and on a beautiful day that spring he led a little troop of the most devoted out into the fields and selected the spot where the New Harmony phalanstery was to be built. The ladies prepared a lunch; the gentlemen cut down a few trees; Mr. Owen made another speech; and everyone joined in singing:

> "Ah, soon will come the glorious day,
>   Inscribed on Mercy's brow,
> When truth shall rend the veil away
>   That blinds the nations now.
>
> "When Earth no more in anxious fear
>   And misery shall sigh;
> And pain shall cease, and every tear
>   Be wiped from every eye.
>
> "The race of man shall wisdom learn,
>   And error cease to reign:
> The charms of innocence return,
>   And all be new again.
>
> "The fount of life shall then be quaffed
>   In peace by all that come;
> And every wind that blows shall waft
>   Some wandering mortal home."

Shortly thereafter, to wipe away whatever tear might still be lingering in whatever eye, Owen called the townspeople together in the Hall of New Harmony on May 9 to give them his rosy "Retrospect" of the first year of the new system of society.

He began by describing the overcrowding of the town. "As soon as the formation of the Preliminary Society was publicly announced," he said, "persons from all quarters crowded into the colony to offer themselves for members; the dwelling houses were filled in two months, and the press for admission was such that it became necessary to put advertisements in the newspapers of the neighboring states to prevent others coming. . . . On my arrival here in January last, I found every room fully occupied."

And now, he went on, "in one short year, this mass of confusion, and in many cases of bad and irregular habits, has been formed into a community of mutual cooperation and equality, now proceeding rapidly to a state of regular organization."

In the splintering process that was taking place, giving birth to the communities of Macluria and Feiba Peveli, founded by dissenters, Owen saw only a multiplication of hopes, not a division among his followers. "Perhaps," he said, "no system of equal magnitude, involving such extensive changes in the conduct of human affairs, ever made progress in any degree approaching to it in so short a time. Hereafter, no one who comes and visits Macluria or Feiba Peveli will doubt the practicability of this scheme."

All in all, he said, the affairs of the society had been managed better than he had expected, and he was not worried by the false rumors that had been spread about it. "The deliverance from poverty and ignorance, and the oppression of riches is at hand," he announced, somewhat ambiguously.

The Fourth of July that year marked the fiftieth anniversary of American independence, but Robert Owen felt a need to give the holiday a greater significance. Once more catching the opportunity to make a speech, he gathered his people into the Hall of New Harmony, and from the platform where Father Rapp had been able only to predict the imminence of the millennium, he announced its arrival.

"As I can not know the present state of your minds," Owen began, solemnly, "and the continuance of my life at my age is very uncertain, I have calmly and deliberately determined upon this eventful and auspicious occasion, to break asunder the remaining mental bonds which for so many ages have grievously afflicted our nature and, by so doing, to give forever FULL FREEDOM TO THE HUMAN MIND."

The capital letters are Owen's, as they appeared in *The New Harmony Gazette* the next week. They seem to testify that his chronic addiction to words had now reached a stage where their effect depended on their size, just as Hollywood was to discover, a century later, that *colossal*, after it has been used a million times, ceases to be bigger than big unless it becomes COLOSSAL.

"I now declare to you," Owen continued, "that Man, up to this hour, has been, in all parts of the earth, a slave to a TRINITY of the most monstrous evils that could be combined to inflict mental and physical evil upon his whole race.

"1. private property

"2. absurd and irrational systems of religion

"3. marriage founded upon individual property combined with some of these irrational systems of religion.

"For nearly forty years have I been employed, heart and soul, day by day, almost without ceasing, in preparing the means and arranging the circumstances to enable me to give the death blow to the tyranny and despotism which, for unnumbered ages past, have held the human mind spellbound, in chains and fetters, of such mysterious forms and shapes, that no mortal hand dared to approach to set the suffering prisoner free. Nor has the fullness of time for the accomplishment of this great event been completed until within this hour—and such has been the extraordinary course of events that the Declaration of Political Independence, in 1776, has produced its counterpart, the DECLARATION OF MENTAL INDEPENDENCE in 1826—the latter just half a century from the former."

At the close, with Jehovah-like finality, he told his audience: "This truth has passed from me, beyond the possibility of recall."

And beyond recall it went. Although the dateline of *The New Harmony Gazette* thereafter read, "First Year of Mental Independence," and a year from that date it began, "Second Year of Mental Independence," nowhere else in New Harmony did the truth that passed from Robert Owen seem to produce any effect. His management of community affairs worsened daily. By the end of the next six months he had "re-organized" the community at least five times—eight times, if William Maclure's count is accurate—and the final shuffle, in January, 1827, was a virtual abandonment of responsibility for the town. In that last "re-organization," Owen proposed to lease his lands to any group or individual who would agree to establish a society upon his principles. It was at this time that William Taylor, the business partner with the ingratiating manner, got hold of the 1,500 acres for his distillery.

Owen's sons, Robert Dale and William, admitted the defeat of the Community of Equality in an editorial in the *Gazette* on March 28, 1827. They still had faith in the principles of Owenism but ascribed the failure at New Harmony to their father's disregard of "the early antisocial circumstances that had surrounded many of the quickly collected inhabitants of New Harmony before their arrival." They pointed out, however, that on the lands of New Harmony, outside the town itself, the community system was "in progressive operation." They went on then to describe what had been accomplished in Macluria, Feiba Peveli, and Community No. 4, and they still cherished hopes of Taylor's good faith on his 1,500 acres.

Meantime, although he was preparing to return to England, Robert Owen continued making hopeful speeches in the Hall of New Harmony; and even when he delivered his two consecutive Farewell Addresses, on May 26 and 27, 1827, he refused to admit defeat. "The social system is now firmly established," he told his listeners in the first of his two farewells. In the second, however, he slipped over into the future tense: "With the right understanding of the principles upon which your change from the old to the new has been made, you will attain your object."

For whatever had gone wrong with the Community of Equality, Owen blamed the New Harmony school system and thus, indirectly, William Maclure, whose province that had been. "If the schools had been in operation upon the very superior plan upon which I had been led to expect they would be . . . it would have been, I think, practicable . . . to have succeeded in amalgamating the whole into a community." At this point, as an earnest of his faith in the superiority of his own ideas about education, he announced that he was giving three thousand dollars for the remainder of the year for the appointment of James M. Dorsey, former treasurer of Miami University in Ohio, who was newly arrived at New Harmony, to start a school of the kind that he, Robert Owen, desired.

Owen left New Harmony June 1, 1827, spent two months in the eastern states describing the "progress" of the social system on the banks of the Wabash, and in late July sailed for England. He was back in the United States the following spring and delivered another lecture in the Hall of New Harmony on the 13th of April, 1828. He returned to the village again in March, 1829; and between the years 1844 and 1847, on his last journeys to the United States, he visited his sons in Indiana frequently. But after his Farewell Addresses of May, 1827, his mind was filled with other schemes and New Harmony no longer held his interest.

19

In the purchase of the New Harmony property, in paying the debts of the community, and in meeting his losses to swindlers, Robert Owen spent about $200,000 of a fortune that was originally more than a quarter of a million. Robert Dale Owen and William Owen gave him their New Lanark shares, worth about $50,000 each, and when he left for England in 1827, he deeded them a $30,000 share in the New Harmony estate in exchange. When he returned in the 1840's, the elder Owen had exhausted his money, and at that time he conveyed the entire New Harmony property to his sons in return for an annuity of $1,500 for the rest of his life.

After his abandonment of New Harmony, one of Owen's schemes was to persuade the government of Mexico to turn over to him the province of Coahuila and all of Texas as a new proving ground for his "system." He expected not only Mexico but the United States and Great Britain to guarantee the independence of the newly formed state. In spite of a discouraging letter from the Mexican minister to England, he set off for Central America armed with a memorial explaining how he would regenerate the world with the aid of the Mexicanos.

En route, Owen stopped in Jamaica and was so impressed by the happy ignorance of Jamaican slaves that he expressed a hope that the abolitionists of England would cease their efforts to free them "until knowledge can no longer be kept from them." With all his humanitarianism, slavery never seemed evil to Owen; equality, as he defined it, did not include equality of the races.

In Mexico, after convincing himself that he had converted

the Bishop of Puebla to his new view of society, Owen went to the capital and saw the President of Mexico and promptly converted him. Or so he thought. Thereafter, he believed he converted General Santa Anna also and, after that, the captain of the American warship that conveyed him to New Orleans. But in New Orleans he discovered, to his great dismay, that he had overlooked the conversion of the Mexican Congress; they were not interested in his plans.

After this abortive revolution, Owen became involved in the Trade Union movement in England and published numerous journals; he called a "World Convention" in New York in 1845 and once more expounded his views; during the revolution of 1848 he was in Paris urging his system upon Lamartine and other revolutionary leaders. Finally, when he was eighty-two, he was converted himself—to spiritualism, by his son Robert Dale—and during the last years of his life he was on intimate terms with Thomas Jefferson, Benjamin Franklin, Shakespeare, Shelley, Napoleon, and the Duke of Wellington. His most frequent companion in this period, however, was the Duke of Kent who had supported his crusade for social justice in his early days. Of the deceased Duke, Owen wrote: "His whole spirit proceeding with me has been most beautiful; making his own appointments, meeting me on the day, hour, and minute he named."

In November, 1858, failing in health, Owen made a visit to his birthplace in North Wales. Newtown had not changed greatly in the three-quarters of a century that he had been away. He put up at a hotel two doors from the house of his birth, and although he was rapidly becoming very ill, he called in the Rector of Newtown and arranged with him for a series of public meetings at which he would present a plan for reorganizing the town's educational system. The next day he died, but not before Robert Dale Owen, the United States minister to Naples, who was fortunately in London at the time, reached his bedside. His body was taken to the house where he was born and thence to the church, from which he was buried in the village churchyard.

Like many dedicated people with a high purpose, Robert Owen was inspired by an all-encompassing sympathy for humanity but was incapable of empathy in his relations with the individuals who composed humanity. Consequently he lacked both a sense of humor and a sense of appropriateness and was an unconscionable though often lovable bore. Macaulay called him "a gentle bore" and fled his company on social occasions, where Owen endlessly expounded his social theories, even at fancy dress balls. Sir Leslie Stephen called him one of those "bores who are the salt of the earth." Harriet Martineau found him a bore, too, and said of him: "Everyone who treated him with respect and interest was assumed to be his disciple; and those who openly opposed or quizzed him were regarded with a good-natured smile, and spoken of as people who had very good eyes, but who had accidentally got into a wood, where they could not see their way for the trees. He was . . . always gentlemanly and courteous in his manners . . . always palpably right in his descriptions of human misery; always thinking he had proved a thing when he had asserted it; and always really meaning something more rational than he had actually expressed." What Miss Martineau complained of most sharply in her nonetheless admiring and affectionate appreciation of Robert Owen was the total absence of reason in his thinking.

Owen was not a philosopher of any substance nor, in the end, a reformer of any specific accomplishment. There were but few ideas in his head, and most of those, although he was unaware of the fact, were secondhand and never completely thought out. He did not know that he was not an original thinker because he was an uninformed man. He read very little, and from the little he read he accepted only what corroborated his own preconceived notions. In other words, he was an unteachable man. He had no sense of the past and no real knowledge of human nature in his own time, beyond his abiding wish that men could live in a better world. His system was unsystematic because it was mere postulation. At New Lanark, his school was conducted on the vaguest of general principles. At New Harmony, his society had no practical organization or direction.

Owen repeated ad infinitum throughout his life that he had arrived at all his "conclusions" through experience, and yet, if his life is looked at either closely or in the perspective of time, it is evident that he was totally lacking in the most essential kinds of experience for the beginning of wisdom: understanding through suffering and learning through trial and error. Born into a time when success in business was almost inevitable for a man of determination, intelligence, energy, and immunity to the temptations of vice—all of which qualities he possessed from childhood—he never knew the meaning of struggle or of failure in the first half of his life; and by the time he was middle-aged he had so confused the word with the deed, the assertion with the proof, that he was incapable of recognizing the need for struggle or the existence of failure when he was confronted with them. He was not a good businessman in the modern sense of the word, for he began his life in a world where the margin of profit was so wide that ultimate riches for a businessman once established were almost inescapable. Thereafter, as William Maclure often pointed out, he followed up his enthusiasm with the force of money. When the money failed to do its work, the experiment failed with it, for he lacked the good administrator's talent for cooperation, compromise, planning, and deliberate and unrelenting effort.

Nor in Owen's personal life was there much evidence of struggle. He did not have to compete. By his own admission, he was the brightest boy in school, in all regards the most promising boy in Newtown. He loved and respected his parents, but it was they who consulted him, not he who consulted them; and when he left home at the age of ten, there is no note of homesickness in his memoirs and no mention of his ever longing to see his parents or his friends in Newtown again. He was completely absorbed in his own life and the immediate world about him. He loved his wife too, but he left her without a qualm in his later years, to follow his dream in America, and he ignored her pleas that he return to her. He dearly loved his children, but when his wife wrote to him that his favorite daughter, Ann, was dying, he was too busy in London curing the ills of the world to come to her bedside or attend her funeral. He was by no means heartless; but he was so obsessed by his *idée fixe* that none of life's accidents and tragedies, short of the total misery of the human race, could disturb his sublime serenity.

Robert Owen was not a true reformer; he was a prophet. He built nothing, but long before anyone else he recognized the inherent disasters that lay waiting for mankind in the social and industrial structure of his day. He hated man's inhumanity to man and willed, most generously and benevolently, to eradicate it; and if he did not succeed in creating the new moral world that he dreamed of, he at least made men aware of the need of it.

As a person, too, Owen was admirable in his never-failing courtesy and kindness. Toward the middle of his life his humanity got lost in his humanitarianism, but until the very end of his life he continued to inspire love and respect even among those whom he bored. He left his wife, but he never abandoned her, and his children adored him and did everything they could to make him happy in his dotage, which came upon him earlier than it comes to most men.

It is unfortunate for the reputation of Robert Owen that he came to America and bought New Harmony when he was fifty-three. Had he died ten years before, his deeds would have approximated his creed and there would have been no shadow on his bright place in history except an untimely death. He would have had a place then among those enigmatic men of the past whose work seems sometimes greater than it was because it was cut short before its completion.

But in spite of the chaos that Owen created in his American Community of Equality, it is fortunate for New Harmony and for America that he came. From his dream he built nothing so tangible and lasting as the works of the German Harmonists who preceded him, but his dream was a lamp whose light they shunned in their dark parochialism. Mental Freedom he called it, and it burned in the town on the Wabash for many years after his departure and illuminated a large area of American history and culture by it burning.

20

Owen's lamp would not have continued to burn in New Harmony—indeed, it might never have got properly lighted—if it had not been for several men and at least one woman with a clearer view of reality than Owen's and with considerably more intellectual substance than he possessed. The woman was Madame Fretageot, who served the cause of the educational experiment in continuous residence longer than anyone else. Among the several men were Owen's sons—William, Robert Dale, David Dale, and Richard—and the naturalists, Thomas Say and Charles-Alexandre Lesueur. But most important of all was William Maclure. Of Maclure, Arthur E. Bestor, Jr., editor of Maclure's and Madame Fretageot's correspondence, justly writes: "In the long perspective of time Maclure's contribution to New Harmony was more enduring than Robert Owen's."

Maclure was born in Ayr, Scotland, in 1763, and was therefore sixty-three years old, ten years older than Owen, when he came to New Harmony. Such details of the Ayrshireman's early life as are recorded may be inaccurate, for they derive from the memory of his brother, Alexander, after William's death in 1840. In the town of Ayr, where the memory of Robert Burns, Maclure's senior by four years, dominates the scene, there is no record of William Maclure's birthplace nor any reminder of his childhood. He is believed to have come to the United States for the first time at the age of nineteen and returned to London as a partner in the English-American mercantile firm of Miller, Hart and Company. Like Robert Owen, he rose fast in his commercial enterprise and made a fortune even larger than the Welshman's. He came to America again in 1796, but was back in Europe in 1803 as a public functionary, settling claims of American citizens against France for losses during the French Revolution. On this mission he traveled widely through Europe and in his spare time collected specimens of natural history to send back to America.

When Maclure came once more to the United States, choosing it as his homeland, he had prepared himself to undertake a geological survey of the country. During the next four or five years, rock hammer in hand, traveling alone afoot and on horseback, crossing and recrossing the Allegheny Mountains some fifty times in his journeys back and forth from the Atlantic coast to the Rockies and from the St. Lawrence River to the Gulf of Mexico, he made geological observations in almost every state and territory in the Union.

Geology was a new science in those days. In fact, it was hardly regarded as a science at all, and the lonely figure of William Maclure breaking rocks with his hammer in remote country was a unique sight that often made woodsmen and mountaineers spread the word that a lunatic was at large in their region. On one occasion, as he approached a public house, his reputation had arrived ahead of him, and the tavernkeeper and his patrons barricaded themselves inside and refused to admit him until they had parleyed with him at length through the windows and convinced themselves that he was harmless. The privations and the hunger and thirst that Maclure survived in his journeying persuaded him to adopt the frugal diet that he lived on the rest of his days. Twenty years later, one of the essays that he published in *The New Harmony Gazette* argues that even the most moderate and sober people eat three times more than they need to.

A memoir of Maclure's accumulated observations on the geology of the United States was published in the *Transactions of the American Philosophical Society* in 1809. But he was not content with this preliminary report. He continued his travels and his samplings of the earth, and in 1817 the American Philosophical Society published an amended and revised report under the title, *Observations on the Geology of the United States of America, with some remarks on the Nature and Fertility of Soils, etc.*

In the preface to this second edition of his *Geology*, Maclure not only expressed his dismay over society's neglect of his particular science up to that time but managed to combine his lamentation and reproof with a characteristic criticism of the social structure: "All inquiry into the nature and properties of rocks, or the relative situation they occupy on the surface of the earth, has been much neglected. It is only since a few years that it has been thought worth the attention of either the learned or the unlearned; and even now a great proportion of both treat such investigations with contempt, as beneath their notice. Why mankind should so long have neglected to acquire knowledge so useful to the progress of civilization—why the substances over which they have been daily stumbling, and without whose aid they could not exercise any one art or profession, should be the last to occupy their attention—is one of those problems perhaps only to be solved by an analysis of the nature and origin of the power of the few over the many."

Subsequent surveys by both the state and federal governments of the United States, completely staffed and manned, better equipped, and well financed, have confirmed the accuracy of the observations Maclure made in his extensive travels alone and unaided. Pamphlets and brochures claiming and advertising "firsts" for New Harmony—the first kindergarten, the first woman's club, etc.—are fond of populating the town with "Fathers": the Father of Infant Education, the Father of American Zoology, the Father of American Ichthyology, etc. Perhaps the New Harmonite who best deserves this kind of title is William Maclure, as the Father of American Geology.

Maclure made his home in Philadelphia, where he watched over the infancy of the Academy of Natural Sciences, founded in 1812, and served as its president from 1817 until his death. The *Journal* of the Academy was begun under his auspices, and a large part of Volume I was printed in his house. After the death of Thomas Say, who was his closest friend, he transferred his library from New Harmony to the library of the Academy, and it was one of his gifts of money that made possible the Hall of the Academy at Broad and George Streets, completed in 1840.

In the winter of 1816–1817, accompanied by Charles-Alexandre Lesueur, Maclure investigated the geology of the West Indies, and in 1819 he went to France and then to Spain, to which he was attracted by the liberal constitution the Spanish Cortes had adopted. In Spain he planned to establish an agricultural school for the working classes, combining physical labor and study, on an estate of 10,000 acres that he purchased outside Alicante. He repaired the buildings of the estate and was ready to open the school when the liberal Spanish government was overthrown and the Church reoccupied the property that had been taken from it. Maclure wanted to stay on in Spain to make a geological survey but was discouraged by the infestation of its remote areas by robbers and kidnapers. In his will, as was learned after his death, he listed alongside his thirty buildings and ten thousand acres in and around New Harmony over a million reales in Spanish securities, a house at Calle del Lobo 7 in Alicante, an estate of ten thousand acres in Valencia, and another near Alicante.

By the time Maclure returned to the United States, Madame Fretageot had aroused his interest in Owen's plans for New Harmony, and he was persuaded to go there with her, taking his friends Say and Lesueur with him, sending Gerard Troost ahead, and later bringing Joseph Neef from Kentucky. He shipped his private collections in natural history and his library to New Harmony by sea from Philadelphia to New Orleans and thence by steamboat to the Wabash town, and for the next ten years they formed a considerable proportion of New Harmony's museum.

Maclure stayed in New Harmony only six months on his first visit. His health was poor and he found the climate of southern Indiana intolerable. He was back in October, 1826, but after seven weeks departed for the warmth of New Orleans. In April, 1827, he returned once more and stayed until the fall of that year to disentangle himself from his relations with Owen. When he left this time, he took Say with him and they traveled together through Mexico all that winter. After the death of Say in New Harmony, William Maclure's brother, Alexander, took charge of his interests there and rebuilt the Rapp-Maclure home when it burned. William Maclure died in Mexico March 23, 1840.

Maclure was a tall, robust, handsome man with red hair and an aquiline nose jutting from his large head. He had a peppery temper and did not tolerate fools easily. Often he was as thorny as the Osage orange that was named for him, *Maclura pomifera,* which Thomas Say brought to New Harmony. He had opinions and theories about almost everything, which he stated dogmatically and often in highly original language. Not all his prophecies have come true; at least, so far, foxes are not looking out the windows of Philadelphia houses as he predicted they would do one day when large cities in America came to their inevitable economic doom, but until the recent restorations in the neighborhood of Independence Hall, that part of Philadelphia that was the heart of the city in his day came very close to the fate he described for it.

Many of his opinions Maclure got off his chest in three volumes published at New Harmony in 1831, 1837, and 1838 under the title, *Opinions on Various Subjects, Dedicated to the Industrious Producers.* Many others he expressed in his badly spelled letters, in which *female,* for example, appears consistently as *famil.* One of these letters, addressed to Say from Mexico, bears testimony in a single paragraph to the size of his head, his theories about diet, and his faith in education.

"Having worn my old fur-cap ever since I left home, and wishing to substitute a Mexican hat with a low crown and broad brim, suited like most of their dresses to protect them from the vertical sun, I searched the shops in Vera Cruz, Jalapa, Puebla, and of this city, but could not find a Mexican hat large enough for my head. Are their heads small, because they have been habituated to make greater use of other parts of their body? For instance their stomachs, which they torture, scarify, and violently stimulate, by the constant application of hot red-peppers, which they call *chille;* which if I may judge from my own experience is the only cause of their stomach complaint, which is so frequent here. . . . If they were to stimulate the head more, and the stomach less, they would most probably have better health of both body and mind."

Maclure believed that climate had a great deal to do with the kind of governments nations chose and argued that "surplus produce, to feed and support the tyrant and his adherents, is the sina qua non of despotism." As proof, he contrasted the tyranny in South America with the freedom of the North American Indians at the time of the discovery of the Western Hemisphere. He was scornful of the American proclivity to imitate European fashions and institutions. He believed small political units had a better chance of survival than large ones. He mistrusted the imagination and said of it, "Our species is the only one that dreams when awake." Although he was very rich, economy was his watchword. "Everything useful is cheapest," he contended, pointing out that walking was the best exercise, water the best drink, plain food the most nourishing, and the most useful knowledge that which is most easily acquired.

By knowledge "most easily acquired" Maclure meant knowledge of the properties of men and things immediately around us. His educational theories were built upon an exclusive faith in the observable. As a child in Ayr, according to his brother, he began his education under a man named Douglass famous in the vicinity for his "classical and mathematical attainments"; but the classical knowledge that Mr. Douglass tried to impart to Maclure had little appeal. From the beginning, he was interested only in what he could see and touch.

Believing that children as well as other animals commence their instruction the moment they begin to make use of their senses, Maclure contended that they should be put into schools at the earliest possible age and, while they studied, should learn to clothe and feed themselves by their own labor. Whereas Robert Owen was noted for his fondness for children, which inspired a friend once to remark to Robert Dale that if his father had had seven thousand children in the Owen family nursery instead of seven there would still have been love enough to go round, William Maclure took a bachelor's more objective view. He argued against the old system of imprisoning children in school four or five hours a day "to a task of irksome and disgusting study," not because of any tender feelings for the little moppets but because, he said, they afterwards were "let loose on society for eight hours, full of revenge and retaliation against their jailors."

Recognizing the difficulty in finding teachers who would devote all their time to their pupils, a consideration that never occurred to Owen, Maclure proposed a school that occupied children with something useful from five in the morning till eight in the evening with such variation of activities that their attention was never fatigued with more than one hour of the same exercise. By "something useful" he meant such subjects as mineralogy, drawing, geology, botany, zoology, and arithmetic. But an extensive study of botany he thought a luxury, and in zoology he would include only those animals that we use for food, that assist us when tamed, and that are, by instinct, led to prey on our property. A knowledge of geography, he believed, was largely a useless burden to the memory, since most of it could be learned, as it was needed, from maps and tables. For literature he found no use at all. "The flowers of rhetoric," he said, "only serve to disguise the truth."

Maclure attributed most of man's misfortunes to the division of society into classes, and insofar as Owen's system would eliminate that division he went along with it. But his purpose in joining the New Harmony experiment was primarily to supervise its educational program. By educating the masses, from infant schools up through agencies for the education of working adults in classes resembling the university extension courses of modern times, he thought he could accomplish more than any revolutionary attempt to reshape society in a single political action. He admired what Owen had done at New Lanark with the Pestalozzian method; with a free hand at New Harmony, he hoped to do even more. He made the costly mistake, however, of not having this division of interests between himself and Owen and the financial terms of their agreement set down clearly in writing at the very beginning of their partnership.

Shortly after the premature organization of the Community of Equality, it became obvious that the educational work of the community could not operate effectively in the social chaos Owen had created; but it was Owen's two oldest sons, not Maclure, who initiated the remedy for shaping the educational experiment into a separately governed group, just as Macluria and Feiba Peveli had broken away. The two sons—Robert Dale and William—were supported by Robert Jennings and by the sympathy, at least, of Madame Fretageot. This schismatic group were known by their opponents in the community as the "Literati."

When Robert Owen refused to tolerate the schism, William Maclure appeared in the debate with a compromise. In the issue of the *Gazette* for May 17, 1826, he proposed that New Harmony be divided into separate autonomous units according to the occupations of its members. This plan appealed to the elder Owen, and in late May the assembly of the society voted itself into three separate groups—the Mechanic and Manufacturing Society, the Agricultural and Pastoral Society, and the Education Society. A lease was then drawn up—the first such formal paper that the two Utopians signed—surrendering to Maclure about nine hundred acres of land for the Education Society. The lease included the Hall of New Harmony, the Steeple House, Community House No. 2, the three-story brick-and-stone granary, and the Rapp mansion.

Apparently Robert Owen still regarded Maclure and himself as full partners in the New Harmony venture, although Maclure did not consider himself involved beyond the Education Society's lease and a liability for half of Owen's losses in the town up to $10,000, which he called a "forfeiture." By August of 1826 Maclure was writing from Cincinnati to Madame Fretageot, in mild reproof: "Mr. Owen, when you mention him as

my partner, I have not the smallest connection with anything he
has done. Every purchase or sale he has made has been either
against my will or unknowing to me, for which I can not for a
moment consider myself responsible. . . . I wish him all the
success possible, tho I'm convinced that a mine of gold would
do nothing towards establishing the community system under
his management. . . . The Schools I shall push to the utmost
extent, but they must be independent of his metaphysics, which
I call all schemes attempted to be introduced into society some
centuries before mankind are prepared for them."

A week later, he was calling Robert Owen "incorrigible"
and counseling Madame Fretageot not to be too quick in following his "visionary schemes." By November 28, he was writing, "My experience at Harmony has given me such horror
for the reformation of grown persons that I shudder when I
reflect having so many of my friends so near such a desperate
undertaking." In February, 1827, he was calling Owen "the
most obstinate man I ever knew," regretting his involvement
in New Harmony, and saying he was sure he could have done
much more good with his property elsewhere. He had at last
become thoroughly disillusioned about his initial admiration
for his fellow philanthropist. "His parot [*sic*] education to ex-
hibit before strangers as at New Lanark is the whole he knows,"
he wrote testily to Madame Fretageot; and, "He is no practical
man himself, nor has he any about him, nor ever can, as the
moment a man is independent to differ from him he discharges
them, and he has nothing but time serving sicofants about him."

When Maclure got back to New Harmony in April, 1827,
Frederick Rapp was there to collect a $20,000 installment on the
purchase price of New Harmony. Rapp also asked for the remaining installment of the same amount at that time, although
it was not due for another year. Owen agreed to the request,
asked Maclure to pay what he regarded as his "partner's" share
of the $40,000, and notified him that he was also liable for some

$90,000 more as a result of the "partnership." Maclure retorted that he owed Owen only $21,000—the $10,000 "forfeiture" to help cover Owen's losses, plus $11,000 for the lease of lands and buildings to the Education Society.

In the end, Maclure paid Frederick Rapp the $40,000 he had come for, but in return he obtained from Rapp the bonds that covered Owen's indebtedness. This made Maclure Owen's creditor, and Maclure immediately filed suit to collect in the Circuit Court of Posey County at Mt. Vernon and simultaneously posted notices about New Harmony warning that he would not be responsible for Owen's debts. Owen countered by posting his own notices to the effect that their partnership was still "in full force" and by filing suit against Maclure for $90,000.

The town was agog. The sheriff came from Mt. Vernon looking for Robert Owen, but Owen eluded him. Soon the word spread throughout the nation that the two Utopians were at each other's throats. But after much recrimination and legal maneuvering, the quarrel was settled out of court and the public was deprived of the spectacle it had looked forward to. Two arbitrators persuaded the litigants to agree on a compromise, Maclure paying Owen $5,000 on his remaining indebtedness and Owen giving Maclure an unrestricted deed to four hundred and ninety acres of New Harmony property in consideration of a sum of $44,000. This deed was recorded on August 23, 1827, and four days later the legal actions in the Posey County Circuit Court were dismissed on the motions of the plaintiffs.

Gradually thereafter community property fell into private hands. James Elliott, James Maidlow, John Cooper, Jacob Schnee (John Schnee's brother), and William Creese Pelham eventually bought most of Feiba Peveli and Macluria, and the factories that the Harmonists had operated communistically with such success fell, one by one, into disuse and were diverted to other purposes. In a letter from New Orleans, dated December 27, 1827—January 3, 1828, Thomas Say wrote to a friend in Philadelphia concerning John Speakman, the former apothecary: "Speakman has indeed turned shepherd, he has purchased the Harmony flock consisting of 8 or 9 hundred, & has removed them to Wanborough, 20 or 30 miles up the river, where with proper attention, he may do well."

As late as 1890, the community names that had survived in the neighborhood of New Harmony, as compiled by several old residents, totaled thirty-four:

Beal, Birkbeck, Bolton, Brown, Cooper, Cox, Dransfield, Duclos, Evans, Fauntleroy, Fretageot, Gex, Grant, Hugo, Johnson, Lichtenberger, West, Lyons, Mumford, Murphy, Neef, Owen, Parvin, Pelham, Pouleybank, Robson, Sampson, Schnee, Snelling, Soper, Stahele, Twigg, Warren, and Wheatcroft.

Today such a count would not produce a dozen, although there are still numerous descendants—like Mrs. Mary Fretageot Hodge and Mrs. Frances Dale Owen Cooper Tanner, for example—who have lost the surname by marriages. Posey County abounds with Owens, but only a few of them are descended from Robert Owen.

Part Three

⋘⋙

And After

21

WITH THE settlement of Owen's and Maclure's misunderstanding and the departure of Owen to larger fields of social experiment, Maclure had a free hand for his reforms in New Harmony. By October, 1828, Robert Dale Owen and Frances Wright removed *The New Harmony Gazette* to New York, renaming it *The Free Enquirer,* and Maclure's *Disseminator of Useful Knowledge* became the official organ of the town. The experiment was thenceforth an educational and cultural experiment only, although social reform was still the ultimate goal.

In 1827, Maclure sent up from New Orleans a printing press for the use of the School of Industry, and it was on this press that the first issue of the *Disseminator* was published, coming out on Wednesday, January 16, 1828. A bimonthly, it was at first a sixteen-page issue in octavo; it changed to quarto in 1832, and finally to folio. Cornelius Tiebout, from Philadelphia, was the printer and engraver, with headquarters at first in the Hall of New Harmony, then in Maclure's home, and afterward in the old Rapp greenhouse. The newspaper had two mottoes: the first was, "Ignorance is the fruitful cause of human misery"; the second, "He who does his best, however little, is always to be distinguished from him who does nothing," a quotation from Dr. Johnson.

Several books were the creation of the *Disseminator's* press. Among them were Maclure's *Opinions,* schoolbooks for use in Mexico, Michaux's *North American Sylva,* and Thomas Say's *American Conchology.* Of the sixty-eight beautiful plates illustrating Say's work, Mrs. Say drew all but the two that were done by C. A. Lesueur. Pupils of the school colored the drawings, Caroline Tiebout earning about two dollars a week at the task, according to a letter from Madame Fretageot to William Maclure dated February 10, 1831.

Robert Dale Owen returned to New Harmony in 1832 and was elected to the Indiana Legislature soon thereafter. The other three sons of Robert Owen had remained in the town and were married in a triple wedding in 1837, William to Mary Bolton and David Dale and Richard to two of Joseph Neef's daughters. William's bride died in the year of her marriage and he survived her by only five years. David Dale and Richard, inspired by William Maclure's collections, became geologists. Madame Fretageot stayed in New Harmony until November, 1831, when she returned to Paris and later joined Maclure in Mexico, where she died in 1833. Thomas Say died in New Harmony in 1834 and was buried on the lawn of the Rapp-Maclure home. Three years later, Lesueur returned to France. Alexander Maclure, William's brother, lived on in New Harmony until 1850. Dying in that year, he was buried beside his two sisters, Anna and Margaret, in Say's vault on the lawn. So, until Maclure's own death, in 1840, when the younger Owens were just beginning to come into prominence as distinguished men in their own right, it might be said that the Scottish geologist was the titular head of the community, at least through his agents and his kin.

When Maclure arrived in New Harmony off "The Boatload of Knowledge," there were more than a hundred children enrolled in the town's already famous schools; in a short while, there were nearly four hundred. Madame Fretageot had about a hundred infants between the ages of two and five under her supervision; Neef and his wife and daughters managed another two hundred between five and twelve; and Phiquepal d'Arusmont had about eighty in the Steeple House learning mathematics and the useful arts. William and Robert Dale Owen assisted in the daily teaching at first, as did Dr. Chase's wife, Martha, called "Patty," whose beauty distracted her male colleagues and the older male students. Say, Troost, and Lesueur gave lectures in natural history, chemistry, and drawing.

Some twenty years before Maclure saw Owen's New Lanark school in operation, he had visited Pestalozzi's school in Switzerland, in 1805, and had become a convert to Pestalozzi's methods. A year later, he sent Neef, one of Pestalozzi's staff, to America, subsidized him while he learned English, and set him in charge of the first Pestalozzian school in this country, near Philadelphia. Later, he put Madame Fretageot in charge of a girls' school in that city. With these two—and with Neef's wife, who had been Neef's pupil in Switzerland, and with Neef's children and Phiquepal d'Arusmont—he had a core of Pestalozzians around whom he could build a dependable staff at New Harmony.

Early in 1826, in Silliman's *American Journal of Science and Arts*, Maclure announced his plans for New Harmony and described the system of instruction his schools would follow. The "great or fundamental principle of education," he explained, was never to try to teach children what they can not comprehend, to proceed always from the known to the unknown, from the easy to the difficult, arriving at conclusions rationally, and avoiding the errors of the imagination. The children were to learn mechanism by machines, arithmetic by an "arithmometer," geometry by a "trignometer." Maclure believed that thus the most useful propositions of Euclid would be reduced to the comprehension of a child five or six years old. Natural history was to be taught by objects or representations of them, anatomy by skeletons and wax figures, geography by globes, etc. He included writing, drawing, and music in the curriculum, but only in elementary and useful forms. No blithe spirit caroled through the refrains sung by the schoolchildren of New Harmony, as witness a poem dedicated to them and published in the *Gazette:*

"Awake! ye sons of light and joy,
 And scout the Demon of the schools:
The fiend that scowls but to decoy,
 To pamper zealots: frighten fools:
To blind the judgment: crib the soul.
 Wake up! And let your actions tell
 That you with Peace and Virtue dwell.

"Away with studied form and phrase,
 Away with cant and bigot zeal,
Let Truth's unclouded beacon blaze,
 From Nature's kindness learn to feel:
From Nature's kindness learn to give
Your hands, your hearts, to all that live.
 Wake up! 'Tis deeds alone can tell
 That you with Peace and Virtue dwell."

Maclure believed the child's mind should not be directed toward any one subject beyond the limits of its span of attention, and therefore no class was to last longer than an hour. To relieve fatigue, he proposed alternating mental efforts with gymnastics, involving of course only such movements of the body "that may lead to utility, such as marching, climbing, the manual exercises, etc." He considered foreign languages important, but believed they should be learned from such fellow students as came to the school from foreign nations. Since he imported several Mexican boys to his school, it can be presumed that Spanish was one of the languages spoken, as was French, learned from the French children who were on "The

Boatload of Knowledge." Finally, manual training would be taught, so that the boys in the school could learn at least one trade.

Since Maclure believed with Owen that corporal punishment should be banned from school discipline, the students of New Harmony were directed toward good behavior by persuasion. The results were not altogether satisfactory. Paul Brown complained of the rowdiness of New Harmony's children, and numerous visitors noted their lack of discipline. In *Threading My Way*, Robert Dale Owen recounts at length how he overcame the unruliness of a boy named Ben without flogging him, concluding, "So I carried my point against a degrading relic of barbarism, then countenanced in England, alike in army, navy, and some of the most accredited seminaries." What Robert Dale Owen failed to note was that, while he was laboriously carrying this point with Ben, the worst-behaved boy in the class was getting the teacher's full attention while the students who were ready to cooperate and to learn marked time awaiting the unruly one's conversion.

Excepting the township schools in New England, there were no public schools in the United States when Maclure undertook the educational experiment at New Harmony, and this was the first public school system open to boys and girls alike. The first public high school in the East for both boys and girls was opened at Providence, Rhode Island, in 1843; the first such school in the West was at Evansville, Indiana, opening in 1854. At New Harmony, Maclure was accepting students of early high school age by 1826. The industrial school that he established was the second in the country, Rensselaer Polytechnic Institute having been founded two years before; and yet Maclure's School of Industry might be called the first trade school, since it offered only manual training and Rensselaer was designed for technicians. In 1828, Maclure undertook a fourth experiment, which he called "the Society for Mutual Instruction," an organization designed to further the education of working adults in their spare time from jobs.

Like Owen, Maclure was more often absent from the scene of his experiments than he should have been for their own good. But there was a difference in that Maclure, who was not himself a teacher, hired and organized a reasonably competent staff to carry on while he was away, whereas, by the very nature of the social experiment, Owen's presence was necessary to its success. For whatever reason, Maclure's educational innovations did not long survive in New Harmony; but they did point the way toward changes in methods of education that have since been widely adopted.

The Indiana Legislature turned Maclure down when he applied for permission to incorporate his Educational Society; but the rejection was the result of his reputation as an atheist and not a rejection of his theories, which were later incorporated into the Indiana school system. Maclure and Owen installed their own free public school system in New Harmony nine years before the state began to support public schools by taxation, and their free public kindergarten and trade school can be called the first in the western world.

An outgrowth of Maclure's "Society for Mutual Instruction" was the Workingmen's Institute and Library, which resulted directly from his correspondence with the workingmen of New Harmony in 1837 through Madame Fretageot's son, Achille. For a number of years, in England and Scotland, laboring men had been organizing clubs for the discussion of social and political problems and for self-improvement in their skills. When such a club was established in New Harmony under Maclure's influence, he gave its members a wing of the Hall of New Harmony as its meeting place and ordered a thousand dollars worth of books from a London bookseller for its library.

When Maclure died, he left by his will "the sum of five hundred dollars to any club or society of laborers who may establish in any part of the United States a reading and lecture room with a library of at least one hundred volumes." One hundred and forty-four such clubs and libraries took advantage of Maclure's beneficence in Indiana, and sixteen more in Illinois were formed, bringing the total distribution of funds from his estate to $80,000 for this purpose. Curiously enough, the Workingmen's Institute did not avail itself of this provision of Maclure's will, although it did later absorb an institute so organized and acquired its three hundred volumes.

Nevertheless, the Workingmen's Institute and Library has survived to this day and still is, as it has been from its inception, one of the most remarkable of small-town libraries in the nation. In the 1870's, when Harmonist agents from Economy tore down the old brick church and built with its bricks the wall that now surrounds their cemetery in New Harmony, they preserved and restored for the library the wing in which it was housed. Twenty years later, another benefactor aided the Institute in the construction of the building which it now occupies.

This latter-day philanthropist was Dr. Edward Murphy. He was born in County Cork, Ireland, in 1813 and wandered into New Harmony in 1826, a homeless, runaway waif, escaping from a brutal man in Louisville who professed to be his uncle. The Owen Community took the boy in, enrolled him in the manual training school, and taught him the printer's trade. For a time, in his youth, Murphy's life took no definite direction. He was a printer, then a tailor, then a farmer. His farm he bought from Robert Dale Owen, and during the transaction he took such a dislike to Owen that he changed his political affiliations and was a vociferous hater of Democrats the rest of his life. He opened a store in a corner of the old Yellow Tavern at Tavern and Main Streets, but this venture soon failed. From commerce he moved on to the study of law and then of medicine, taking courses in Louisville. The practice of medicine finally made money for Dr. Murphy in New Harmony, and the money, put out at interest, made more money. Soon he was rich.

Edward Murphy had married Celeste Johnson of Vincennes when he was nineteen. They had eight children, but the children all died before they reached manhood or womanhood. In the Murphys' later years, they traveled widely in Europe and brought back copies of old masters from Italy, with which Dr. Murphy filled the Institute's art gallery. In 1899 he gave the Institute $45,000, and the next year $31,000. The provisions of his will, when he died without heirs in December, 1900, brought the total of his gifts to the Institute to $155,000.

Today, as a result of William Maclure's inspiration and beneficence, the beneficence of Dr. Murphy and other New Harmony citizens, and the able direction of the officers and librarians of the Workingmen's Institute throughout its century and a quarter of existence, the library of New Harmony houses in its own spacious building more than 18,000 volumes plus priceless manuscripts and records of both the Owen and Rapp communities. It has also kept files of local newspapers and of notes on local history covering almost every aspect of the town's life since the early days.

22

One of New Harmony's local historians, Clarence P. Wolfe, has called the years following the departure of Owen and Maclure "the golden age of New Harmony." Others have referred to it as "the afterglow." Another way to describe what happened to New Harmony from 1830 on to the end of the century is to visualize Owenism on the Wabash as the explosion of a rocket and the varied subsequent activities of Owen's descendants and of other New Harmonites as the shower of sparks that follows a rocket's bursting. None of the sparks was of the brightness or magnitude of the original flash, and in their scattering there was no central brilliance upon which the historian's eye can focus, such as the "Community" of Owen's and Maclure's time. Each went its own way, eccentric and alone; and yet, together, they created an "afterglow" above the town's life that kept it unique in the Middle West, and indeed in the nation, for a long time.

While the spirit of William Maclure assured the cultural survival of New Harmony in the years immediately following the failure of Owen's venture in communism, from the start Owen's children dominated the town's social life and eventually, supported by other "first families," kept the fame of the village on the Wabash alive by their own accomplishments. Their presence attracted many noted visitors to New Harmony. Alexander Philipp Maximilian, Prinz zu Wied-Neuwied, spent the winter of 1832–1833 in the town, attended by his faithful servant, hunter, and taxidermist, Dreidoppel, and accompanied part of the time by his official artist, the young Swiss painter Karl Bodmer. Audubon was in and out, the ornithologist who kept a store in Henderson, Kentucky, nearby. And in the winter of 1845–1846, the Scottish geologist, Sir Charles Lyell, came and noted, among other things, that there was no church in New Harmony but was pleased to find what he described as "a singular phenomenon in the New World, a shy child."

(Once, when New Harmony was chided for its lack of churches by the citizens of Evansville twenty miles away, the New Harmonites retorted that they also had no "shops for the sale of spiritous liquors." Today there are a half-dozen churches in New Harmony, but there are also a couple of bars, although they sell only beer and wine. As for New Harmony children, the shy and the bold alike are protected every school day by ropes across Tavern Street shutting off traffic, so that they can cross in safety to the Library of the Workingmen's Institute. This they do, during recess and after school, in rather phenomenal numbers; at least they are not shy about reading—which is a good thing, and in the tradition of their forbears.)

According to Robert Owen's wish, all five of the Owen families of the second generation lived in one house for a while after their marriages. This home, known as "The Mansion," stood at the eastern edge of town and was for many years the center of community social life and much of the town's intellectual activity. The two-story house was of great size, a hundred and twenty-five feet across the front, with two halls, two front doors, and two front porches. It had a vast garret, and above the open passage that connected the main part of the house to the south wing was a billiard room. Old inhabitants of New Harmony, describing the house after it was torn down, remembered that its fireplaces used a hundred cords of wood a winter and that on the west lawn of the house the swing, for the many Owen children, was hung on timbers forty feet high.

William Owen, David Dale Owen, and Richard Owen were married in a triple ceremony in 1837. Two years before that wedding, Jane Dale Owen had married Robert Henry Fauntleroy, who came to New Harmony from Virginia and, with William Taylor as a partner for a time, operated the community store. Three years before the Fauntleroy-Owen marriage, Robert Dale Owen and Mary Jane Robinson were wed in New York City in a ceremony that attracted even wider public attention than the subsequent triple wedding of Robert Dale's brothers. In the course of time, these five Owen marriages produced nineteen children, fifteen of whom survived past the age of twenty-one.

All of Robert Owen's sons were romantics. Richard had married first, at eighteen, the disturbingly attractive schoolteacher, Patty Chase, who had been previously married to Dr. Samuel Chase. She died, insane, shortly after she became Richard's bride, and nine years later he married Anne Eliza Neef. Family legend, recorded by Caroline Dale Snedeker, David Dale Owen's granddaughter, has it that Anne Eliza's sister, Caroline Neef, fell in love with David Dale Owen when she was a child, and that David Dale had a kind of "Byronic" handsomeness. But Robert Dale Owen's romances were the most exotic of all.

For several years after he came to America, he was faithful to the memory of the laboring man's daughter he had left behind in Scotland, the girl he called "Jessie" in the autobiography he wrote in his seventies; but by 1831 the girl had married and his heart was free. It was probably in that year that Robert Dale Owen's future wife first saw him and, like his mother, Caroline Dale, thirty-five years earlier in Scotland and his sister-in-law, Caroline Neef, in New Harmony later, fell in love with her future husband before he was aware of her existence. While Robert Dale Owen was editing *The Free Enquirer* in New York, he was giving numerous public lectures, and after one of these lectures, eighteen-year-old Mary Jane Robinson told her mother that, although the speaker was the homeliest man she had ever seen, he was the only man she would ever consider marrying. All the early Owens, except "Byronic" David Dale, inherited their father's big nose and generally homely features, but they seemed nonetheless attractive to women.

It was not their romance, however, that made Robert Dale Owen's and Mary Jane Robinson's wedding a public sensation; it was their marriage contract. This agreement, published back home in the *Disseminator* and widely publicized in the newspapers of the East, reads as if it had been written for public consumption as well as private understanding between bride and bridegroom:

"This day, April 12, 1832, I enter into a matrimonial engagement with Mary Jane Robinson, a young woman whose opinions in all important subjects, and whose mode of thinking and feeling, coincide more intimately with my own than do those of any other individual with whom I am acquainted.

"We contract a legal marriage, for we desire a tranquil life in so far as it can be obtained without sacrifice of principle. We have selected the simplest ceremony which custom and the laws of the State recognize, and which involves not the necessity of calling in the aid of a member of the clerical profession—a profession the authority of which we do not recognize, and the influence of which we are led to consider often injurious to society. . . .

"Of the unjust rights which in virtue of this ceremony an iniquitous law tacitly gives me over the person and property of another, I cannot legally, but I can morally, divest myself. And I hereby earnestly desire to be considered by others as utterly divested, now and during the rest of my life, of any such rights —the barbarous relics of a feudal and despotic system soon destined in the course of improvement to be wholly swept away and the existence of which is a tacit insult to the good sense and good feeling of the present comparatively civilized age. . . .

"ROBERT DALE OWEN

"I gratefully concur in these sentiments.

"MARY JANE ROBINSON"

Inevitably, considering the age in which this ceremony took place, the publicity it received, and the cry of atheism that had been raised throughout the country after the retreat of Robert Owen from New Harmony, Robert Dale Owen was accused of advocating "free love," although he had no such intention.

Following a wedding trip abroad, the Robert Dale Owens came to New Harmony to make their home, and four years later, elected as a Democrat to the Indiana Legislature, young Owen set to work to win for other women the independence in marriage that he had given to his own wife. A large majority of the Legislature defeated his bill providing separate property

Rapp-Maclure home, 1914

David Dale Owen's laboratory

Fauntleroy home

Joseph Neef home

Opera House, formerly
Community House No. 4

Wagons of Captain Alfred
Ribeyre, "the Corn King"

New Harmony Centennial parade

(Don Blair)

Golden Rain Tree, also called the Gate Tree in New Harmony

Restored Harmonist house

The Roofless Church

(James K. Mellow)

Mrs. Kenneth D. Owen
and Paul Tillich at the
dedication of Tillich Park

(Robert Lee Blaffer Trust)

rights for married women, but eventually he succeeded in removing from the statute books the law that gave a widow only a life-tenancy of one-third of her husband's real estate. For this "feudal" law he substituted a law that awarded the widow absolute ownership of that proportion of her husband's property.

As Harmonie had sent Frederick Rapp to Indiana's first Constitutional Convention in 1816, so New Harmony sent Robert Dale Owen to its second, in 1850. Here again Owen took up the battle for women's rights, but here again he failed in large part. However, in the course of his services to the state, he put on Indiana's law books legislation that gave it a rank in the vanguard of states that recognized women as human beings. Through his efforts, not only were widows assured of absolute ownership of property inherited from their husbands but married woman gained the right to own and control separate property and to keep their earnings. Owen also got the divorce laws changed to protect women against habitually drunken and abusive husbands. In 1851, in the Hall of the Indiana State House, the women of Indiana presented to their advocate a silver pitcher acknowledging their gratitude and placed at one of the entrances to the capitol a bronze bust of their hero.

Robert Dale Owen similarly fought the battle of free public education in the Indiana Legislature and at the state's second Constitutional Convention, and he was also an ardent advocate there and throughout the nation of the rights of the Negro. In 1862, he wrote an eloquent letter to Abraham Lincoln, who himself had spent fourteen years of his boyhood and youth in southern Indiana only fifty miles from New Harmony. "Can you look forward to the peace of our country," Owen began, "and imagine any state of things in which, with slavery still existing, we would be assured of permanent peace? I cannot. . . ." Secretary Chase later reported that this letter influenced the President more than any other correspondence he received at that time and strengthened him in his ultimate decision to issue the Emancipation Proclamation.

Robert Dale Owen's concern for the Negro is especially remarkable when it is considered against the background of his life. His predecessor at constitutional conventions, Frederick Rapp, had shown no interest in bringing Indiana into the Union free, and his father, Robert Owen, with all his fervid humanitarianism, was stone-blind to the evils of slavery and saw no place for Negroes in a community of equality. There were a few Negroes in the German Harmonists' community, and, later, Joseph Fauntleroy, older brother of Robert Henry Fauntleroy, brought some with him from Virginia; but they lived apart in a home called "the Spencer House," which became a sort of Negro hotel for steamboatmen and for visiting persons of the black race.

For a while there were a few Negroes in the public school of New Harmony, but since 1890 the town has been a "white town," with one brief exception. That exception was a Mrs. Eliza McFarland, whom Harry T. Schnee brought from Owensboro, Kentucky, about 1912 to work in his hotel as a cook. Mr. Schnee, who was a grandnephew of the postmaster of "Owenite" times, had just bought Community House No. 3, known in New Harmony by that time as "The Tavern" because it had been the town's hotel for many years. Eliza McFarland worked and lived in the hotel for a number of years unmolested by the townspeople, but her successor and a Negro man, who came to serve as the hotel's chauffeur, were run out of town by a mob the first night after their arrival. The next day New Harmony's newspaper published an account of the event in a disgracefully gloating and supercilious tone.

Immediately preceding Abraham Lincoln's brief membership in the U.S. House of Representatives, Robert Dale Owen served two terms in that body, from 1843 to 1847. As a Congressman, he drew up and introduced a bill that created the

Smithsonian Institution. From 1852 to 1858, he was American chargé d'affaires and minister in Naples. It was in Naples that he was converted to spiritualism, at a séance in the house of the Brazilian minister; and according to Caroline Dale Snedeker, the Robert Dale Owens' return to New Harmony thereafter was a great trial to his numerous relatives, especially to his brother David Dale, the one son of Robert Owen who remained an atheist throughout his life. David Dale carefully protected his children against the "subversive" stories that their Uncle Robert's children delighted in telling them about the spirit world. Since David Dale's family had moved from "The Mansion" to the Rapp-Maclure house by this time, the quarantine of his children against his brother's notions was not so difficult as it might have been earlier when all the Owens lived in the same house.

Like his father, Robert Dale Owen was a peripatetic reformer, unable to stay long in one place. The rest of his life he was in and out of New Harmony, but he never remained there long at a time. He died at Lake George, New York, in 1877, a year after his second marriage, to Lottie Kellogg. Sixty years after his death, his remains were brought to New Harmony and placed beside his first wife's grave in the Maple Hill Cemetery, south of town.

Jane Dale Owen Fauntleroy too moved early out of the Owen family house. Her husband died in 1850 of yellow fever while on a business trip in the South, and Mrs. Fauntleroy, in a "Rappite" frame house on West Street that is still known as "the Fauntleroy Home," undertook the education of her children and some of her nieces and nephews. Her oldest child, Constance Fauntleroy, went abroad with the Robert Dale Owens and was educated in Europe. When she returned, she organized in her mother's house in 1859 a woman's literary club called the Minerva Society, and her Uncle Robert Dale wrote its constitution.

Frances Wright had organized a Female Social Society in New Harmony in 1825; and so, whether the Minerva Society can rightly be called the first woman's club in America or not, New Harmony can claim the distinction of being the scene of the first female endeavor of that sort. The Indiana Federation of Women's Clubs, however, claims this particular "first" for the Minerva Society, and having bought the Fauntleroy Home in 1919 and maintained it as a museum for awhile, they exercised a kind of squatters' right to the title which it would be ungallant to deny. The Fauntleroy Home is now owned by the Conservation Department of the State of Indiana.

Certainly the Minerva Society was the first full-fledged woman's club in America of the modern variety, complete with motto ("Sapienta Gloria Corona Est"), badge, constitution, officers, and a requirement that each member bring a notebook to meetings. The organization lived for four years, expiring with the meeting of September 28, 1863, at which, according to the minutes of that date, one lady declaimed *The Ocean,* by Byron, "rather fast," another recited *Christ Stilling the Tempest,* which struck the secretary as "rather pie-crusty" and "imperfectly memorized," and Rosamond Dale Owen, Robert Dale's youngest daughter, aged sixteen, closed the exercises with a composition of her own called *Dreams,* which the secretary found "quite original" but "rather short." Brevity, apparently, was not recognized as a virtue at the Minerva gatherings.

David Dale Owen, the third of Robert Owen's sons, was for a while a pupil of Benjamin West in London, but by the time he came to New Harmony with his brother Richard in 1828, he had decided that he lacked sufficient talent to be a painter. His second choice of careers was medicine, and he earned an M.D. at the Miami Medical College in Ohio. But the sight of physical suffering was too much for his sensitive artist's temperament and he soon abandoned the practice of medicine for geology and turned to a study of the collections of William Maclure. David Dale Owen used his medical science often, however, when he led geological surveying parties into remote country, and after the death of Joseph Neef, in 1854, he employed his surgical skill to remove a rifle ball from his father-in-law's head. The old man had received the wound at the Battle of Arcole in Italy in 1796. He always wanted to know where the bullet was in his head and he told David Dale to find it after his death, saying, "You will know it in my stead." The ball rested above Neef's jaw.

David Dale Owen lived out his latter days quietly in the Rapp-Maclure house with his wife and four children, working in the laboratory that he set up in the old brick-and-stone granary behind the house on Granary Street and, afterwards, in the new laboratory that he built for himself behind the granary, facing Church Street. David Dale Owen's "Laboratory" is a charming house, somewhat resembling Braxfield, the Owen countryseat near New Lanark where its builder grew up. Curiously and ornately towered, gabled, turreted, and corniced, it stands apart from the Württembergers' architectural plainness that surrounds it and rivals the Rapp-Maclure house by this distinction. Today it is the New Harmony home of Kenneth Dale Owen, also a geologist, a great-great-grandson of David Dale Owen's father.

After making a preliminary geological survey of the state of Indiana, David Dale Owen was appointed United States Geologist in 1839, and New Harmony was the headquarters of the U.S. Geological Survey for the next seventeen years. In his official capacity, Owen surveyed the Northwest. When Robert Dale Owen got funds appropriated for the Smithsonian Institution, David Dale Owen went to Washington and helped draw the plans for the building. With the removal of the U.S. Geological Survey's headquarters to Washington, he undertook the work of State Geologist for Kentucky and, afterwards, for Arkansas. During the last two years of his life, he was State Geologist of Indiana. He died in New Harmony in 1860.

Richard Owen, younger than David Dale, served as his brother's assistant in his youth and eventually became Indiana's State Geologist himself. For a while he was a teacher of Natural Science in a military school in Kentucky and then part-owner of a school in Nashville, Tennessee. With the outbreak of the Civil War he joined the Federal Army, having served once before as a Captain in the 16th U.S. Infantry in the War with Mexico. At the beginning of the Civil War, he was stationed at Indianapolis in charge of Confederate prisoners taken at Fort Donelson. His kindness in this command was remembered by his charges long after the war, when they placed his bust in the state capitol with a plaque expressing their gratitude. Following this tour of duty, Colonel Owen was at Vicksburg with Grant and was himself captured, but he was released without parole and re-entered the service.

Retiring from the army in 1864, Richard Owen was for the next fifteen years a Professor of Natural Science at Indiana University in Bloomington, where a building was named for him. In 1872, he was elected the first president of Purdue University and served for two years during the period of its organization but never took up residence in West Lafayette or drew a salary.

In the Purdue presidency, Owen's principal duty was to draw up a plan of organization for the new university, and this he did while continuing his teaching at Bloomington and during the summer of 1873 in New Harmony. The plan Owen conceived was widely attacked. One letter writer to the *Indiana Farmer,* signing himself "Humbug," protested against the requirement of military training in Owen's curriculum. "In the name of my grandfather's horn-plow handles," he wrote, "what need of military drill, when there is plenty of peaceful farm work to healthfully develop every muscle of the body?" Because Richard Owen recommended student government in the new university on the grounds that he had seen the system work well in Europe, the letter writer exclaimed, "May the continent perish with dry rot and England be affected with 'hollerhorn'!" Because the new president proposed chemistry, physics, mathematics, English literature, and language as necessary to prepare graduates for directorships of farms and factories, "Humbug" threw up his hands in despair. "Now by all the teeth of a Norwegian harrow," he wrote, "I cannot see in this list where a young man could be fitted for taking charge of anything."

When this letter was reprinted in the *Lafayette Journal*, Owen made the mistake of answering it. Immediately he found himself in the center of a public storm. The trustees of Purdue rejected his plan, and he then engaged in a series of letters trying to obtain some recompense for his labors, pointing out that they had not hesitated to pay an architect for plans that they were not using. Meantime, at Indiana University, where Owen was much loved by his colleagues and students, the university authorities offered him curatorship of the museum in addition to his professorship in order to keep him on the Bloomington campus. Owen resigned his Purdue title in the spring of 1874. He served at Indiana University five years longer, finally retiring when deafness caused by sunstroke made further teaching impossible.

Richard Owen lived eleven years thereafter in New Harmony, receiving and calling on friends, studying and writing, and giving lessons in French and dancing to the children of the town who were sent to his home by their parents. Like most old people, he grew very much concerned about his diet and health, and in his last years he weighed in ounces and recorded in his diary every particle of food that he ate. It was this valetudinarianism that caused his death in his eighty-first year. He had been in the habit of dropping in at A. H. Fretageot's store every evening to drink a glass of "medicated water" with the son of the original Achille. Next door was a hardware store operated by W. W. Robb. Mr. Robb was also an undertaker. One day he ordered some embalming fluid on Mr. Fretageot's stationery and the shipment was sent to Fretageot with the "medicated water." Both Owen and Fretageot drank a glass of Robb's embalming fluid by mistake on the evening of March 24, 1890. Mr. Fretageot survived, but Richard Owen died that night.

23

William, the second of Robert Owen's sons, did not live long enough to carve a name for himself as large in American history or in the annals of New Harmony as the names of his three brothers, but his interest in dramatics brought a distinction to the town throughout the nineteenth century that it might not otherwise have enjoyed. In 1828, William founded the Thespian Society, which gave a vitality to the theatre in New Harmony that lasted almost a hundred years.

In its beginnings, the Thespian Society was fortunate in having the artist, Charles-Alexandre Lesueur, as its stage and scenery designer in the Hall of New Harmony, where the society produced its first plays. Several of Lesueur's paintings were used over and over again, and the backdrop for *William Tell* was preserved for fifty years. In addition to two early productions of *William Tell*, less ambitious dramas were performed by the Thespians, such as *No Song, No Supper* and *The Magpie*. For *The Magpie* Lesueur made birds that actually flew down on the stage and stole things. In 1840, the Thespians produced Robert Dale Owen's one dramatic effort, *Pocahontas,* which had already enjoyed a run at the Park Theatre in New York. In this play, there was too much long-winded parleying between Colonists and Indians for good dramatic effect, but the loyal New Harmonites loved it and were greatly moved by Captain Newport's description of Pocahontas's beauty.

The Joe Jeffersons, father and son, appeared in New Harmony in 1838 when the younger and later more famous Jefferson was only nine years old; and many other itinerant stage celebrities were attracted to the town. For a while, showboats tied up at the New Harmony landing, the most popular being *The Ark* and, later, *The Floating Palace.* But the local theatre was itself so vigorous that there was little need for visiting talent. In 1838, a floating theatre was built at New Harmony and some of the Thespians themselves took to the road—or, more accurately, to the river. They got halfway down the Mississippi before they became dissatisfied with river life and returned to their own stage.

The Thespians' second theatre was the upstairs ballroom of Community House No. 1, which stood on what is now the rear lawn of the Workingmen's Institute Library. The actors used this building till 1854, when they bought Community House No. 4, on Church Street between Brewery and East, tore out its interior floors and partitions, installed a new main floor of yellow pine brought from Florida for that purpose, and erected a stage at the north end of the building. This stage measured twenty-two by twenty-six feet and was fifteen feet high. Peter Duclos, who had helped decorate the St. Charles Theatre in New Orleans, designed the scenery.

Seven hundred seats were set up on the new floor. They were removable, so that the building could be used as a ballroom as well as a theatre. The gallery at the south end seated another two hundred, making Union Hall, as the building was then called, the second largest theatre in Indiana. It retained that rank until the movie palace came into being in the twentieth century, a remarkable distinction, since New Harmony's population never went much above one thousand and neighboring communities like Evansville, Vincennes, Terre Haute, and Indianapolis, were full-grown cities.

Plays were produced in Union Hall as late as 1912, when the Lilley Stock Company came to town for a stand of several nights; but the next year the building was sold and became a garage. It still stands on Church Street—once a "Rappite" and then an "Owenite" dormitory for men, later a tenement house, and for sixty years a lively theatre—and at its north end the outlines of the old stage are still visible.

The Golden family contributed more to New Harmony's fame in the theatrical world than any other of its citizens. Martin Golden, born in Sligo County, Ireland, in 1835, and brought to America at the age of seven, came to New Harmony in 1860. He had already played in *The Hunchback* five years before. He brought his wife, born Emma Isabelle Llewellyn in London in 1842, and later known on the stage as Bella Golden. They organized a traveling troupe of actors and soon they had a son, Martin T. Golden, who traveled with them. Another son, William Echard Golden, born in 1865, was for a time principal of the New Harmony school, but he was a playwright long before that. At the age of eleven, he composed a play entitled *The Masked Ball, or the Rose-Colored Domino,* which was produced by the children of New Harmony. Among his later plays, more widely recognized if not so precocious, were *Benedict Arnold, The Prince of Mantua, Hortense,* and *Bluebells.*

The Goldens tried out many of their plays in New Harmony's Union Hall, among them *"The Gilded Age,"* before they took them on the road into Ohio, Kentucky, Illinois, and other parts of Indiana. Their daughter, Frances Golden, made a hit in the child's part in *East Lynne,* billed as "Little Fanny." Another daughter, Grace Golden, became the prima donna of the

Castle Square Opera Company and achieved a national reputation. She was born in the Fauntleroy Home on West Street in 1867, where the Goldens lived for a while after they moved into the town.

Another name associated with New Harmony's later years is that of Josiah Warren, an inventor from Boston. Warren had been in New Harmony in the days of Owen's community but left after its dissolution to establish a "Time Store" in Cincinnati. In 1842, he returned to New Harmony and opened a similar store there.

Using Robert Owen's idea of labor notes, Warren added them to the cash paid for merchandise in his store as payment to the merchant for his services. He charged cash for the goods at cost and received in addition a note recording the buyer's further indebtedness for service in the store. Such a note might be worth a half hour of carpentering or plowing or five pounds of Indian corn, that being estimated the product of one half-hour's labor. The store was thus a labor exchange that eliminated the middleman. It worked for a while, but the complicated bookkeeping that was required consumed too much of Warren's time and energy, and he could not long survive in competition with more conventionally operated establishments.

Warren was more successful with his inventions, especially his speed press, which was the first to print a newspaper on a continuous sheet. While he was at New Harmony, he received seven thousand dollars for some of his patents. He bought land then near the town to set up a Utopia of his own but abandoned that neighborhood for what he considered a more favorable site in Ohio. Later he moved to Long Island and founded The Village of Modern Times on his principles of commercial equality.

Not all the nineteenth-century New Harmonites were Utopian idealists, however. Some came and grew fabulously wealthy on the fat land of Posey County. One of these was John Ribeyre, who arrived from France in 1848, about the time of the Revolution of that year. A native of Severac in the department of Aveyron, he and his French wife spoke with the accent of the Midi. Before he died, in 1893, he is said to have acquired property in the county worth half a million dollars. His son, Alfred Ribeyre, inherited the father's business acumen. Alfred, known as Captain Ribeyre and self-crowned "The Corn King," decorated the side of one of New Harmony's Main Street buildings with his royal title and also painted all his farmhouses a brash yellow to distinguish them from those that owed him no fealty. At one time, early in the present century, the gentle Posey County countryside was blistered with hundreds of such houses and outbuildings.

By continued association with New Harmony, either as residents or as frequent visitors there among their many relatives, several Owens of the third and fourth generations have kept the intellectual and spiritual sparks of the town flying well into the twentieth century. One was the novelist, Caroline Dale Snedeker, descended from Robert Owen through the David Dale Owen line. Her story *The Town of the Fearless* is a warm and intimate account of Neef and Owen family life in Switzerland and Scotland and on the Wabash shore. Another is Grace Zaring Stone, descended from Robert Dale Owen, well known in modern times as the author of *The Bitter Tea of General Yen* and, under the pseudonym of Ethel Vance, the exciting story *Escape*.

Most exotic of the latter-day Owens—and more in the tradition of her reforming forbears—was Rosamond Dale Owen, youngest daughter of Robert Dale Owen. She lived from 1847 until 1937. Author at sixteen of the composition *Dreams* that closed the last meeting of the Minerva Society, Rosamond Dale led an active, peripatetic, adventurous life but never failed to keep pen in hand. Her autobiography, *My Perilous Life in*

Palestine, published in 1929, tells more about herself than most ladies in their eighties are inclined to tell.

Rosamond Dale Owen married first Sir Laurence Oliphant, the English social reformer. When Sir Laurence proposed marriage, he told Miss Owen that she had forgotten "the mission of women to be beautiful," that, in fact, his first wife had been much better-looking than she was. But Rosamond had "a noble head," said he, and she suited him well enough, since, on principle, he preferred to forego the physical relationship with her in marriage, just as he had done in regard to his first wife. Rosamond agreed to this condition, said she was willing to serve him only as a handmaiden to the memory of the first Mrs. Oliphant, and the bond was sealed. Sir Laurence was fifty-nine at the time; Rosamond was forty-two; Sir Laurence survived the ceremony by only a few months.

Next, Rosamond Dale Owen Oliphant married a disciple of Sir Laurence's on the same chaste basis. Murray Templeton had not been previously wed, but a girl in Scotland who thought herself engaged to him was giving him a lot of trouble. In spite of this difficulty, Templeton and Mrs. Oliphant went ahead with their plans. Within a year after the platonic nuptials, Templeton fell overboard from a ship and was drowned while crossing the Mediterranean, and Rosamond Dale was a widow once again.

The rest of her life, Rosamond Dale Owen Oliphant Templeton engaged in litigation with the Turkish government over possession of a thousand acres near Haifa that she had inherited from Sir Laurence. The land encompassed Armageddon and the site of King Solomon's stables, and the point of the dispute, so far as it can be determined from the litigant's confusing accounts of the matter, was whether the land was what the Turks called *Mushā'a* (land held in common with others) or *Mafruda bi-at-Tapu* (land separated and allotted to an individual through

the agency of the Turkish land registration office). Mrs. Templeton's title was not cleared till the year of her death at her home
in England.

Rosamond Dale Owen's early "dreams" developed into heav-
enly visions, which she enjoyed the rest of her life along with
a morbid fear of men. According to her autobiography, everywhere she went strange men were given to staring at her in
public with evil thoughts in their heads. Her first discovery
of the wickedness of the male came when she was seventeen.
On a train ride from Evansville to Cincinnati, she was placed
in the care of an elderly German of Evansville. All the way to
Indianapolis, where they had to change trains, the old German
sat decently apart from her at the far end of the car, but at Indianapolis, in a blinding snowstorm, he persuaded her that the
Cincinnati train connection could not be made and he put her
up in a shabby hotel. (En route to Indianapolis, she had discouraged the advances of a gentleman in the seat behind her
who, she decided later, must have been John Wilkes Booth.)

At four o'clock in the morning, just as seventeen-year-old Rosamond had been expecting all night, the elderly German came
to her hotel room, and at once it was obvious to her that he
had been indulging in a few beers.

"A Power greater than my own strengthened me," she wrote
sixty years later; "and I continued to look him straight in the
eyes, until he shrank from my gaze and backed towards the
door."

In his retreat, however, the German managed to tell her
that he had only come to announce that it was time to go to the
station and catch the Cincinnati train.

The experience aged Rosamond Dale ten years, she said; but
her sudden access of maturity did not prevent her making a
scene among her friends in Cincinnati that required the German to do a lot of explaining when he got back to Evansville.

Beginning with a hatred for the word sex, which she considered appropriate to "women of the austere type," Rosamond Dale Owen, in her autobiography, described her feelings about this subject at length in a chapter which she entitled "Sex." In this chapter, mulling over experiences with men that had brought her more than once to the brink of a fate worse than death, the twice-married authoress arrived at a theory not unlike the theory chastely espoused by the Württemberg Harmonists a century before. Through abstinence from sexual relations, she decided, men and women could prepare themselves for a day when they could no longer be given in marriage because they would be "one and undivided as in the Male and Female Image of God."

During the first fifty years of the present century, except for one brief flurry of welcome to the outside world in 1914 when the town's Centennial was celebrated, New Harmony dozed in the sun in summer and withdrew itself against the raw unpredictable weather of its winters. In mid-June each year, the townspeople observed with a festival the blooming of the Golden Rain trees, descendants of the tree that William Maclure sent from Mexico to Thomas Say and that Say planted by the gate of the Rapp-Maclure home, thus giving the raintree the name "gate tree" in New Harmony. In August, for several decades, "The Great Posey County Fair" brought the town briefly to life again. But for the most part, New Harmony lost its touch with the world.

In the Library of the Workingmen's Institute, faithful attendants kept the local annals up to date in card catalogues and watched over the "Rappite" and "Owenite" manuscripts and publications in their care. Old folks sat on their front porches and talked about the Golden Age. Arthur E. Fretageot, Madame Fretageot's great-grandson, kept something of the spirit of Community days alive by allowing the young people to dance in old Community House No. 2 every Saturday night. And in the schoolhouse, behind the doorway of the golden rose that

Frederick Rapp had carved, children continued to learn the story of their town and take pride in it. But too many of those children never came back to New Harmony after they went to college, and at home the members of the old families grew older and died. In spite of the Workingmen's Institute, the dances, the Fauntleroy Home, the "Rappite" museum of the Colonial Dames, a brief effort of a state memorial commission with insufficient funds and very little cooperation from the townsfolk, and the continued existence of many architectural reminders of the past, the old tradition of intellectual vigor and unconventional plans for the world's improvement was dying out in New Harmony as the Owens, the Fretageots, the Pelhams, the Fauntleroys, the Elliotts, the Murphys, and the Goldens either diminished in number or vanished entirely from the scene.

Kenneth Dale Owen was one of those who left New Harmony when he was young. Like so many of his ancestors, he was a geologist, and eventually he became a successful consultant in Houston, Texas. He kept a home in New Harmony, however, and when he married Jane Blaffer he brought her back to see his hometown and she saw its neglected possibilities. What Mrs. Owen has done since in the town on the Wabash with her own money and with funds from the Robert Lee Blaffer Trust that she established is not altogether in the tradition of the Utopians led by George Rapp and then by Robert Owen, except that, like their endeavors, it is highly original in concept and execution.

While Kenneth Owen bought the David Dale Owen "Laboratory," the brick-and-stone granary, and the Rapp-Maclure home and made of their acreage a new Owen enclave in the heart of the town, Mrs. Owen bought and "restored" many brick and frame houses of the "Rappites." It is necessary to enclose the word "restored" in quotation marks, because Mrs. Owen has moved some of the houses to new sites, painted some with colors that would have shocked the Württembergers, and christened them with names unrelated to New Harmony's history—

"the Poet's House," "the Pink Cottage," "the Gate House," and at least one "Community House" that was originally a private dwelling.

Mrs. Owen has built a "Roofless Church" at the north edge of town, between Main and West Street, well accommodated obviously to the convenience of descending angels should any henceforth choose to appear on the banks of the Wabash. Designed by Philip Cortelyou Johnson, it is a walled garden, one hundred and thirty feet wide by two hundred and thirty feet long, in the center of which rises a fifty-foot dome of laminated pine arches. Beneath this dome is a bronze designed by Jacques Lipchitz, on which, in French, an inscription reads, "Jacob Lipchitz, Jew, faithful to the religion of his ancestors, has made this Virgin to foster understanding between men on earth that the life of the spirit may prevail." Two other castings of this bronze are on Iona, an island in the Hebrides, and in the church of Notre Dame de Toute Grâce of Assy, France. On May 1, 1962, ceremonies at the Roofless Church dedicated ornamented gates to the entrance, also designed by Lipchitz. The following year, on June 2, 1963, Mrs. Owen brought Professor Paul Johannes Tillich to New Harmony to speak at the dedication ceremonies of a small park across the street from the church, which she has named Tillich Park. In this park she is constructing a "Cave of the New Being," the design of Frederick Kiesler. The subject of Professor Tillich's address on the occasion of his appearance in New Harmony was "Estranged and Reunited: The New Being."

Mrs. Owen's dream, as she has described it for the press, is of a cultural awakening, basically mystical and religious, that will have New Harmony as its center. Her ceremonies and dedications include processions, liturgical and secular music, and the presence of clergymen of various denominations in the lively social gatherings of artists, writers, and musicians that she imports for these occasions from New York and abroad. She installs apprentice poets, painters, and musicians in her various houses philanthropically in the hope that they will derive inspiration from the atmosphere of New Harmony in their creative efforts, and she has employed a clergyman as her full-time cultural and spiritual overseer in the town. Whether a cultural revival can be so superimposed upon a Hoosier village that for fifty years or more has not felt altogether at ease with strangers is a question yet to be answered. But whatever the answer, New Harmony is once more unique.

Not so very long ago, you could go to New Harmony by train, from Evansville, if you were willing to rise before dawn and spend three or four hours on a journey of some twenty miles as the crow flies, with a layover and change of cars at Stewartsville and, finally, a ride of about a mile in a hack to the center of town. It has been a longer time since the town could be approached by boat, as George Rapp's and Robert Owen's followers approached it when they came to find paradise in the wilderness. Passenger service on the Wabash came to an end soon after Jenk Hugo ran the *Juno* aground at New Harmony in the 1860's and inadvertently formed an island with her hulk. Today, if you want to go to New Harmony, you must go by road, in a bus or car.

The time to go is in June or October. In June, the Trees of the Golden Rain are in bloom, and in October the beech and maple and gum and hickory are aflame in the blue haze that rises like smoke from the river. In midsummer New Harmony is often scorched by the sun, and in winter it can be dismal and gray.

The winding and often dog-legged roads from the northeast will take you across the whole breadth of Posey County, Indiana's southernmost county and one of its mellowest and most Hoosier, and will let you discover before you arrive that your journey is measured in years as well as miles, in timelessness as well as time. At the end of the journey, you will find that in

AND AFTER

New Harmony it is both yesterday and today, with now a note of tomorrow recently added, and that the town lives wholly in none of these three worlds. Indeed, if you listen closely, you may hear the faint flutter of angels' wings in the drowsy sunlight, and if you look closely, knowing New Harmony's story, you may see signs of that old serpent, which is the Devil and Satan, as the Book of Revelation says. Both the angel and the serpent have visited the little town on the Wabash and they still return occasionally, as they always do wherever men and women dream too passionately of perfection on this earth.

Appendix
Bibliography
Index

The Memorial of George Rapp and the Harmony Society, 1806

To his Excellency
 THOMAS JEFFERSON, Esquire
  President of the United States of America
 The Memorial of George Rapp & Society of Harmony in Butler County Respectfully sheweth:
  First, the Reason of their Emigration to America,
  Second, their concerns in that place where they live presently, and
  Third, their purpose of purchasing a quantity of Land of the United States.
 Your Memoralists are natives of the Electorate of Würtemberg in Germany, and have been there in corporated to the Lutheran Religion after the Law of the Country yonder; having become acquainted through the Grace of God Enlightening of the holy Spirit with the decline of Christianism since Eighteen Years, so they was going the Way of Piety, after the sense of Jesus, and formed a proper Community, the Number of which now amount to Two thousand men; having been persecuted & punished in many manner for sake of the Truth which they perceived and confessed, they was necessitated to look for a place, where is liberty of Conscience, & where they

may exercise unprevented the Religion of the Spirit of Jesus. Your Memoralists understanding by the History of the United States, America would be such a place, the whole Society was unanimously resolved to send their Leader George Rapp accompanied with some brethren before them, to inquire about the Country; after whose notice are already in Phila & Baltimore arrived about fourteen hundred men, which body of People consists of Tradesmen, Farmers and chiefly cultevators of the Vine, which last occupation they contemplate as their primary Object, and whilst they know how to plant and prepare Hemp & Flax, having good Weavers among them, so they are intended to erect too a Linen Manufactory. Whereas the Culture of Vine requires a peculiar climate & soil, Your Memoralist George Rapp has Eighteen Month ago been travelling in the Western part of this Country, on the North side of the River Ohio, in quest of a suitable Situation for this body of People & their purposes, where he had found a piece of Land, thirty Miles north of the Ohio, & about Eighty Miles west of Pittsburgh, which Land he understood is the property of the United States, and which he had flattern Reasons to believe will answer to the objects in view of his fellow Country men, however when he was travelling back to Philadelphia to expect the ships with his Friends, an other bought the best Section out of said Land which he had choosen—and if they were gone further back into the Woods, they would have put themselves in a Distance of 60-80 miles from all settlements about, which they would not venture, out of warning and counsel of many experienced men; thereof thereupon they bought four thousand five hundred acres of Land in Butler County in a Distance of 26 miles of Pittsburgh, for two Dollars a half pr. acre.

The Society engreases dayly, and after the Letters Your Memoralists have got lately from Germany, they expect as much men more as are here already. The Land where they live presently is too small, too brocken & too cold for to raise Vine. Your

Memoralists can not whether hit to their aim in Cultivating
Vineyards nor extend themselves, On account of this Your
Memoralists Respectfully solicit from the Government to grant
them a quantity of about Thirty thousand Acres of Land (more
or less, as the Government will deem it) in the western Country, where Your Memoralists will choose a suitable piece of
Land for their purposes, if the Government will grant.

Your Memoralists beg to represent, that when they was selling their Houses and Property in Germany, they got Scarce
half the value of it; that they had large Expences of Travel by
Land & Sea, having a good deal unwealthy People among them
for which they paid fright, that they bought their Lands above
mentioned by Cash, that they spended much Money by regulat-
ing of their Households after the greatest Exigence, that they
Bought Cattles for two thousand Dollars and that they had a
whole Year to buy Victuals for about Nine hundred Men, in
that manner their Estate has been diminished, they can not pay
directly the Land for which they supplicate, they therefore
Respectfully Solicit from the Government To allow them a
Terms of four, eight and twelf Years. After three or four Years
Your Memoralists will be able to pay thereon about, twelf or
fifteen thousand Dollars. The whole Society does bind themselves as long as there shall be any property among them. Your
Memoralists hope that the Government will deem it good Pol-
icy, and be desposed to encourage and Emigration so valuable,
as they flatters themselves, this will prove to their Country.

Finally, Your Memoralist deem it incumbent on him further
to represent, that he left a good Deal members of his society
in Germany, desiring support of the Society, to be brought too
to America, but finding it impossible to undertake too unwealthy a Charge, most of them being indigent Circumstances,
he found it necessary to decline such Overture, but he deem it
his duty to represent the Case to the Government, and if it
should see Cause to engage the needed but honest and indus-

trious People on their arrival in this Country, That Your Memoralist will all those associated with him are willing to be bound to the United States for any advance it may judge right to make them. All of which is Respectfully submitted.

The Second Harmonist Contract, 1821

(AUTHORIZED TRANSLATION)

Be it hereby known that today, '20th January, 1821,' in the year of our Lord, one thousand eighteen hundred and twenty-one, the present agreement, treaty and alliance was made and concluded between us, the following persons to wit: N. N. etc., of the one part and George Rapp and his associates of the other part.

After the aforesaid persons become sufficiently acquainted with the principles, rules and regulations of the community of George Rapp and his associates, by virtue of their religious principles, they have, after long and mature reflection, out of their own free will, determined to join the community of said George Rapp and his associates, in Harmonie, Posey County, State of Indiana; to that purpose the aforesaid persons bind themselves and promise solemnly by these presents, to comply with the ordinances, rules and regulations of the community, and render due obedience to the superintendents ordained by the community and to perform as much as possible all occupations and labors to which they are ordered, and help promote the benefit, happiness and prosperity of the community. And if the case should happen that the aforesaid persons, jointly or singly, after a short or long period of time, leave the community for any cause whatever, they hereby bind themselves jointly and each for himself separately, never and in no case to bring any account, or make any claim, either against the association, or any individual member thereof, for their labor and services rendered; also, never to make any demand, ask or claim any other payment, under any name and description whatsoever, but will do and have done all things out of Christian love, for the good and benefit of the community, or else take it as a gift, if George Rapp and his associates willingly give them something.

However, George Rapp and his associates, in return, adopt the aforesaid persons into the community, whereby they obtain prerogative to partake of all meetings for divine services by which they receive in church and school the necessary instructions, requisite and needful for their temporal benefit and happiness, and eternal felicity. George Rapp and his associates bind themselves further to supply the aforesaid persons with all the wants and necessaries of life, to wit: Meat, drink, and clothing, etc., and indeed not only during their healthful days, but also if all or any of them get sick or otherwise infirm and unable to work, they shall, as long as they remain members of the community, receive and enjoy the same support as before during their better days, or as their circumstances require.

SELECTED BIBLIOGRAPHY

Albjerg, Victor Lincoln. *Richard Owen: Scotland 1810–Indiana 1890.* (Archives of Purdue, No. 2.) Lafayette, Ind.: Purdue University, 1946.

Andressohn, John C. "The Arrival of the Rappites at New Harmony," *Indiana Magazine of History,* XLII (December, 1946), 395–409.

———. "Twenty Additional Rappite Manuscripts," *ibid.,* XLIV (March, 1948), 83–108.

———. "Three Additional Rappite Letters," *ibid.,* XLV (June, 1949), 184–188.

[Annals of Congress.] *Debates and Proceedings in the Congress of the United States, 1789–1824.* 42 vols.; Washington, D.C., 1834–56. 9th Cong., 1st sess., 1805–1806.

Ashton, T. S. *The Industrial Revolution, 1760–1830.* London: Oxford University Press, 1948.

Banta, Richard E. "New Harmony's Golden Years," *Indiana Magazine of History,* XLIV (March, 1948), 25–36.

Bernhard, Karl, Duke of Saxe-Weimar Eisenach. *Travels Through North America, during the years 1825 and 1826.* 2 v. in 1; Philadelphia: Carey, Lea & Carey, 1828.

Bestor, Arthur E., Jr. *Backwoods Utopias: The Sectarian and Owenite Phases of Communitarian Socialism in America, 1663–1829.* Philadelphia: University of Pennsylvania Press, 1950.

——— (ed.). "Education and Reform at New Harmony: Correspondence of William Maclure and Marie Duclos Fretageot, 1820–1833," *Indiana Historical Society Publications,* 15, No. 3 (1948), 283–417.

Birkbeck, Morris. *Notes on a Journey in America, from the Coast of*

Virginia to the Territory of Illinois. Philadelphia: Caleb Richardson, 1817; London: Ridgway and sons, 1818.

Blair, Don. *The New Harmony Story.* Mt. Vernon, Ind., n.p., 1959.

Blane, William. *An Excursion through the United States and Canada during the years 1822–1823. By an English Gentleman.* London: Baldwin, Cradock, and Joy, 1824.

Boewe, Charles. "The Manuscripts of C. S. Rafinesque, 1783–1840," *Proceedings of The American Philosophical Society,* 102, No. 6 (1958), 590–595.

Bole, John Archibald. *The Harmony Society.* Philadelphia: Americana Germanica Press, 1904.

Brinton, Crane. *A History of Western Morals.* New York: Harcourt, Brace, 1959.

Brown, Paul. *Twelve Months in New Harmony.* Cincinnati: William Hill Woodward, 1827.

Brown, Samuel R. *The Western Gazetteer; or Emigrant's Directory.* Auburn, N. Y.: H. C. Southwick, 1817.

Buley, R. Carlyle. *The Old Northwest: Pioneer Period, 1815–1840.* 2 vols.; Bloomington: Indiana University Press, 1950.

Byrd, Cecil K. "The Harmony Society and *Thoughts on the Destiny of Man,*" *The Indiana University Bookman,* I (January, 1956), 5–15.

Call, Richard Ellsworth. *The Life and Writings of Rafinesque.* (Filson Club Publications, Vol. X.) Louisville: 1895.

Calverton, V. F. *Where Angels Dared to Tread.* Indianapolis: Bobbs-Merrill, 1941.

Carter, Clarence Edward (ed.). *The Territory of Indiana, 1800–1810.* (*The Territorial Papers of the United States,* Vol. VII.) Washington, D.C.: Government Printing Office, 1939.

Chinard, Gilbert. "The American Sketchbooks of C. A. Lesueur," *Proceedings of The American Philosophical Society,* 93, No. 2 (1949), 114–118.

Cobbett, William. *A Year's Residence in the United States of America.* (Third part contains Thomas Hulme's Journal of a Tour in the West.) London: Sherwood, 1818–19.

Cole, G. D. H. *Robert Owen.* Boston: Little, Brown, 1925.

BIBLIOGRAPHY

Cox, Sandford C. *Recollections of the Early Settlement of the Wabash Valley.* Lafayette, Ind.: Courier, 1860.

Dana, Edmund. *Geographical Sketches on the Western Country Designed for Emigrants and Settlers.* Cincinnati: Looker, Reynolds, 1819.

Davidson, Marshall B. "Carl Bodmer's Unspoiled West," *American Heritage,* XIV (April, 1963), 43–65.

Denehie, Elizabeth Smith. "The Harmonist Movement in Indiana," *Indiana Magazine of History,* XIX (June, 1923), 188–200.

Duclos, Victor Colin. "From the Diary and Recollections of Victor Colin Duclos. Copied from the original manuscript by Mrs. Nora C. Fretageot," *Indiana Historical Collections,* III (1916), 536–547.

Duss, John S. *George Rapp and his Associates.* Indianapolis: The Hollenbeck Press, 1914.

———. *The Harmonists, A Personal History.* Harrisburg, Pa.: The Pennsylvania Book Service, 1943.

Elliott, Helen. "Development of the New Harmony Community with Special Reference to Education." Unpublished Master's thesis. Indiana University, 1933.

Faux, William. *Memorable Days in America.* London: W. Simpkin and R. Marshall, 1823.

Flint, Timothy. *Recollections of the Last Ten Years, Passed in Occasional Residence and Journeyings in the Valley of the Mississippi.* Boston: Cummings, Hilliard, 1826.

Flower, George. *History of the English Settlement in Edwards County, Illinois.* (Chicago Historical Society Collections, Vol. I.) Chicago, 1882.

Fordham, Elias Pym. *Personal Narrative of Travels in Virginia, Maryland, Pennsylvania, Ohio, Indiana, Kentucky; and of Residence in the Illinois Territory: 1817–1818.* ed. Frederic Austin Ogg. Cleveland: Arthur H. Clark, 1906.

Forster, William. *Memoirs of William Forster.* ed. Benjamin Seebohm. 2 vols.; London, 1865. Extracts relating to Indiana in *Indiana Historical Collections,* III (1916), 250–268.

Fretageot, Nora C. *Historic New Harmony: A Guide.* New Harmony, n.p., 1934.

BIBLIOGRAPHY

Fritsch, William A. *German Settlers and German Settlements in Indiana.* Evansville, Ind., n.p., 1915.

Gedanken über die Bestimmung des Menschen. Attributed to George and Frederick Rapp. Harmonie: The Harmony Society of Indiana, 1824.

Hamy, E. T. "Les voyages du naturaliste Ch. Alex. Lesueur dans l'Amérique du Nord, 1815–1837," *Journal de la Sociéte des Américanistes de Paris,* V (1904).

"The Harmonists," *Atlantic Monthly,* XVII (May, 1866), 529–538.

The Harmony Society in Pennsylvania. Federal Writers' Project. Philadelphia: William Penn Association of Philadelphia, 1937.

Harvey, Rowland Hill. *Robert Owen, Social Idealist.* Berkeley: University of California Press, 1949.

Hays, George A. *Early American Printing and the 1822 Harmony Wood Press.* Old Economy, Pa., n.p., 1961.

———. *Founders of the Harmony Society.* Old Economy, Pa., n.p., 1959.

———. *Gertrud Rapp.* Old Economy, Pa., n.p., 1959.

Hebert, William. *A Visit to the Colony of Harmony, in Indiana in the United States of America.* London: George Mann, 1825.

Hendrickson, Walter Brookfield. *David Dale Owen, Pioneer Geologist of the Middle West.* (Indiana Historical Collections, Vol. XXVII.) Indianapolis, 1943.

Hertzler, J. O. *The History of Utopian Thought.* New York: Macmillan, 1923.

Hinds, William Alfred. *American Communities.* Oneida, N.Y.: American Socialist, 1878.

History of Posey County, Indiana. Chicago: Goodspeed Publishing Co., 1886.

Holliday, John H. "An Indiana Village, New Harmony," *Indiana Historical Society Publications,* 5, No. 4 (1914), 201–229.

Holloway, Mark. *Heavens on Earth: Utopian Communities in America, 1680–1880.* London: Turnstile Press, 1951.

Hurst, Roger A. "The New Harmony Manuscript Collections," *Indiana Magazine of History,* XXXVII (March, 1941), 45–49.

Indiana, A Guide to the Hoosier State. Writers' Program of the

Works Projects Administration. New York: Oxford University Press, 1941.

Jordan, David Starr, and Butler, Amos W. "New Harmony," *Scientific Monthly*, XXV (November, 1927), 468–470.

Journal of the Senate of the United States, 1806. 5 vols.; Philadelphia and Washington, D.C., 1820.

Kettleborough, Charles. *Constitution Making in Indiana*. (Indiana Historical Collections, Vols. I, II.) Indianapolis, 1916.

Knoedler, Christiana F. *The Harmony Society, a Nineteenth-Century American Utopia*. New York: Vantage Press, 1954.

Knox, Julia LeClerc. "The Unique Little Town of New Harmony," *Indiana Magazine of History*, XXXII (March, 1936), 52–58, 282.

Krebs, Albert. "L'Oeuvre de C. A. Lesueur Peintre-Naturaliste," *Revue de la Porte Océane*. Le Havre, 1951.

Lang, Elfrieda. "The Inhabitants of New Harmony according to the Federal Census of 1850," *Indiana Magazine of History*, XLII (December, 1946), 355–394.

Leopold, Richard William. *Robert Dale Owen*. (Harvard Historical Studies, Vol. XLV.) Cambridge, Mass.: Harvard University Press, 1940.

Lesueur, Charles-Alexandre. "Voyage en Amérique" (manuscripts and sketches). Vols. 1–6. Muséum d'Histoire Naturelle du Havre.

Lindley, Harlow (ed.). *Indiana as Seen by Early Travelers*. (Indiana Historical Collections, Vol. III.) Indianapolis, 1916.

Lockridge, Ross F. *The Old Fauntleroy Home*. New Harmony: New Harmony Memorial Commission, 1939.

Lockwood, George B. *The New Harmony Movement*. New York: D. Appleton, 1905.

Loir, Mme Adrien. *Charles-Alexandre Lesueur: artiste et savant français en Amérique de 1816 à 1839*. Le Havre: Muséum d'Histoire Naturelle, 1920.

Macdonald, Donald. "The Diaries of Donald Macdonald, 1824–1826," *Indiana Historical Society Publications*, 14, No. 2 (1942), 143–379.

Maclure, William. *Opinions on Various Subjects, Dedicated to the Industrious Producers*. New Harmony: Printed at the School Press, Vol. I, 1831; Vol. II, 1837; Vol. III, 1838.

———. "An Epitome of the Improved Pestalozzian System of Education, as practiced by William Phiquepal and Madam Fretageot, formerly in Paris and now in Philadelphia, communicated at the request of the editor," *American Journal of Science and Arts*, X, No. 1 (1826), 145–151.

Macmillan, Kerr D. *Protestantism in Germany*. Princeton: Princeton University Press, 1917.

Martineau, Harriet. *Biographical Sketches, 1852–1875*. 4th ed.; London: Macmillan, 1876.

Maury, André. "Charles-Alexandre Lesueur, Voyageur et Peintre-Naturaliste Havrais," *French-American Review*, I, No. 3 (July–September, 1948), 161–173.

———. *L'Oeuvre Zoologique de Charles-Alexandre Lesueur*. Le Havre, 1962.

Maximilian, Alexander Philipp, Prinz zu Wied-Neuwied. *Travels in the Interior of North America*. Translated from the German by Hannibal Evans Lloyd. London: Ackermann, 1843.

Moody, Richard. *America Takes the Stage*. Bloomington: Indiana University Press, 1955.

Morton, Samuel George. *A Memoir of William Maclure, Esq*. Philadelphia: Academy of Natural Sciences, 1841; 2nd ed., Merrihew & Thompson, 1844.

Nevin, D. E. "The Late George Rapp and the Harmonists," *Scribner's Monthly*, XVII (March, 1879), 703–712.

"New Harmony," *The Lilly Review*, 22 (July–August, 1962), 12–17.

The New Harmony Gazette, October 1, 1825–October 22, 1828.

Nordhoff, Charles. *The Communistic Societies of the United States*. New York: Harper & Bros., 1875.

Noyes, John Humphrey. *History of American Socialisms*. Philadelphia: Lippincott, 1870.

Owen, David Dale. "Regarding Human Foot-Prints in Solid Limestone," *American Journal of Science and Arts*, XLIII, No. 1 (1842), 14–32.

Owen, Robert. *The Life of Robert Owen, by himself*. New York: Knopf, 1920.

———. *A New View of Society*. London: R. Watts, 1817; Longman,

BIBLIOGRAPHY

Hurst, Rees, et al., 1817. New York: E. Bless & E. White, 1825.

Owen, Robert Dale. *Threading My Way: Twenty-Seven Years of Autobiography*. London: Trübner, 1874. New York: G. W. Carleton, 1874.

Owen, William. "Diary of William Owen from November 10, 1824, to April 20, 1825," ed. Joel W. Hiatt, *Indiana Historical Society Publications*, 4, No. 1 (1906), 1–134.

Packard, Frederick A. *The Life of Robert Owen*. Philadelphia: Ashmead & Evans, 1866.

Parrington, Vernon L., Jr. *American Dreams; A Study of American Utopias.* ("Brown University Studies," Vol. 11.) Providence, 1947.

Pears, Thomas and Sarah. "New Harmony: An Adventure in Happiness," ed. Thomas Clinton Pears, Jr., *Indiana Historical Society Publications*, 11, No. 1 (1933), 1–96.

Pelham, William. "Letters to William Creese Pelham, 1825 and 1826," *Indiana Historical Collections*, III (1916), 360–417.

Pence, George, and Armstrong, Nellie C. *Indiana Boundaries: Territory, State, and County.* (Indiana Historical Collections, Vol. XIX.) Indianapolis, 1933.

Pinson, Koppel S. *Pietism as a Factor in the Rise of German Nationalism.* (Studies in History, Economics and Public Law, No. 398.) New York: Columbia University Press, 1934.

Podmore, Frank. *Robert Owen, a Biography.* 2 vols.; New York: D. Appleton, 1907. London: Hutchinson, 1906.

Rafinesque, C. S. *A Life of Travels and Researches in North America and South Europe, or Outlines of the Life, Travels, and Researches of C. S. Rafinesque.* Philadelphia: F. Turner, 1836.

Rodman, Jane. "The English Settlement in Southern Illinois, 1815–1825," *Indiana Magazine of History*, XLIII (December, 1947), 329–362.

Sargant, William Lucas. *Robert Owen, and His Social Philosophy.* London: Smith, Elder, 1860.

Schneck, J., and Owen, Richard. *The History of New Harmony, Ind.* Evansville, Ind.: Courier Co., 1890.

Schoolcraft, Henry R. "Remarks on the Prints of Human Feet observed in the secondary limestone of the Mississippi Valley,"

BIBLIOGRAPHY

American Journal of Science and Arts, V, No. 2 (1822), 223–231.
————. *Travels in the Central Portions of the Mississippi Valley.*
New York: Collins and Hannay, 1825.
Sears, Louis M. "New Harmony and the American Spirit," *Indiana Magazine of History,* XXXVIII (September, 1942), 225–230.
"Sketch of the Life of David Dale Owen," *American Geologist,* IV (August, 1889), 65–72.
Snedeker, Caroline Dale. *The Town of the Fearless.* Garden City: Doubleday, Doran, 1931.
Thomas, David. *Travels Through the Western Country in the Summer of 1816.* Auburn, N.Y.: David Rumsey, 1819.
Trollope, Mrs. Frances. *Domestic Manners of the Americans.* ed. Donald A. Smalley. New York: Knopf, 1949.
Tyler, Alice Felt. *Freedom's Ferment: Phases of American Social History to 1860.* Minneapolis: University of Minnesota Press, 1944.
Vail, R. W. G. "The American Sketchbooks of a French Naturalist, 1816–1837," *Proceedings of the American Antiquarian Society,* N.S., XLVIII (1938), 49–155.
Warden, D. B. *A Statistical, Political, and Historical Account of North America.* 3 vols.; Edinburgh: A. Constable, 1819. Philadelphia: T. Wardle, 1819.
Weiss, Harry B., and Ziegler, Grace M. *Thomas Say: Early American Naturalist.* Springfield, Ill.: American Antiquarian Society, 1931.
Welby, Adlard. *A Visit to North America and the English Settlement in Illinois.* London: J. Drury, 1821.
Williams, Aaron. *The Harmony Society at Economy, Penna.* Pittsburgh, n.p., 1866.
Williams, Mentor L. "Paulding Satirizes Owenism," *Indiana Magazine of History,* XLIV (December, 1948), 355–365.
Wilson, William E. *On the Sunny Side of a One Way Street.* New York: Norton, 1958.
————. "Pioneers in Paradise," *Holiday,* XV (June, 1959), 42–47.
————. *The Wabash.* (The Rivers of America Series.) New York: Farrar and Rinehart, 1940.
Winchell, N. H. "A Sketch of Richard Owen," *American Geologist,* VI (September, 1890), 135–145.

BIBLIOGRAPHY

Wolfe, Clarence P. *The Story of New Harmony.* New Harmony: The Commercial Club, 1930.

Woods, John. *Two Years' Residence in the Settlement on the English Prairie.* London: Longman, Hurst, Rees, Orme, and Brown, 1822.

Young, Marguerite. *Angel in the Forest: A Fairy Tale of Two Utopias.* New York: Reynal & Hitchcock, 1945.

Young, Otis E. "Personnel of the Rappite Community of Harmony, Indiana, in the year 1824," *Indiana Magazine of History,* XLVII (September, 1951), 313–319.

INDEX

INDEX

INDEX

INDEX

INDEX